STUDY GUIDE
to accompany

MARRIAGE AND THE FAMILY
DIVERSITY AND STRENGTHS
Second Edition

Jeanne Kohl
University of Washington

Mayfield Publishing Company
Mountain View, California
London • Toronto

Copyright © 1997 by Mayfield Publishing Company

All rights reserved. No portion of this book may be reproduced in any form or by any means without written permission of the publisher.

International Standard Book Number: 1-55934-658-2

Manufactured in the United States of America
10 9 8 7 6 5 4 3 2 1

Mayfield Publishing Company
1280 Villa Street
Mountain View, California 94041

CONTENTS

To the Student   iv

Part I: Introduction

    Chapter 1   Perspectives on Intimate Relationships   1
    Chapter 2   Cultural Diversity: Family Strengths and Challenges   13
    Chapter 3   Understanding Relationships in Marriage and Family   25

Part II: Developing Intimate Relationships

    Chapter 4   Friendship, Love, and Intimacy   37
    Chapter 5   Singlehood, Dating, and Mate Selection   49
    Chapter 6   Sexual Intimacy   61

Part III: Dynamics of Intimate Relationships

    Chapter 7   Gender Roles and Power in the Family   75
    Chapter 8   Communication and Intimacy   87
    Chapter 9   Conflict and Conflict Resolution   99
    Chapter 10   Managing Economic Resources   113

Part IV: Stages of Marriage and Family Life

    Chapter 11   Cohabitation, Marriage, and Early Married Life   125
    Chapter 12   Parenthood   137
    Chapter 13   Midlife and Older Couples   149

Part V: Challenges and Opportunities

    Chapter 14   Family Stress and Coping   161
    Chapter 15   Family Problems, Domestic Violence, and Alcohol Abuse   173
    Chapter 16   Divorce and Adjustment   187
    Chapter 17   Single-Parent Families and Stepfamilies   199
    Chapter 18   Strengthening Families in the Future   211

TO THE STUDENT

This Study Guide has been written to help you get the greatest possible benefit and enjoyment from the course in which you are using *Marriage and the Family: Diversity and Strengths,* by David H. Olson and John DeFrain. This Guide is designed not only to assist you in mastering the information in each chapter of the textbook but also to suggest ways of applying that information to your own life.

For each chapter in the textbook, the Study Guide contains several parts. To help you review and understand the main ideas in each chapter and prepare for examinations and quizzes, each chapter has four related components: the Outline of the chapter; a review of the Learning Objectives for the chapter; a fill-in key terms review; and practice test items. The test items include multiple-choice, true/false, and short answer questions. An answer key appears at the end of each chapter.

The second objective of this Study Guide is to provide opportunities for you to address, on a personal level, topics of high interest and application to intimacy, marriage, and family. To accomplish this objective, each chapter contains a Personal Involvement Assessment and a Knowledge in Action Exercise. Each assessment and exercise is designed to serve as a practical and private guide for values clarification and insight into how new information can affect our lives through application.

The Personal Involvement Assessment provides an opportunity to examine one specific issue in depth. You may, for instance, be asked to apply your views on gender stereotypes (Chapter 2) or your views about the problems experienced by singles (Chapter 5), how well you take criticism from others (Chapter 9), or what you know about child sexual abuse (Chapter 15). Each issue included relates directly to concerns most expressed by students in this course.

Finally, the Knowledge in Action Exercise highlights a key research study on one specific topic introduced in the textbook chapter. Following a restatement of the research finding or issue, you are asked to apply it to a "real-life" situation involving others. Having learned something about how cultural conflict within a family is related to different values (Chapter 2), you may be asked to conduct an interview with another student who has a different cultural background or sexual orientation, as part of constructing a family life history. In Chapter 8, the project is to record conversations and analyze them for potential gender differences in communication styles of males and females. The Knowledge in Action Exercise for Chapter 16 is to visit and record the perspectives of the principals, the children, and witnesses in a divorce or child custody court.

The amount of time and effort you give to the material in this Study Guide will depend on your own motivation and on what your instructor requires. If you use the Guide as a parallel reading with the textbook, you will find that it enables you to identify and remember important themes and concepts of each chapter, consistently score better on exams and quizzes, and most important, apply what is learned in the course to your personal life.

We wish to thank Frank Graham for his editorial guidance. The authors, David H. Olson and John DeFrain, have written an impressive introduction to marriage and the family that is both intellectually stimulating and personally relevant to every person who reads it. This Study Guide would not have been possible except for their efforts.

CHAPTER 1

PERSPECTIVES ON INTIMATE RELATIONSHIPS

CHAPTER OUTLINE

Realities of Marriage and Family Life
    Marriage and the Family Are Changing
    Why Do So Many Marriages End in Divorce?

Defining Marriage and Family
    What Is a Family?
    What Is Marriage?

Trends in Marriage and the Family: Change and Continuity
    Trends in Family Structure
    Trends in Marriage
    Trends in Divorce and Remarriage
    Continuity in Marriage and the Family

Conceptual Frameworks for Studying Marriage and the Family
    Family Systems Theory
    The Family Strengths Framework
    The Family Development Framework
    The Symbolic Interaction Framework
    The Feminist Framework

Family Science: An Emerging Profession
    A Knowledge Explosion
    Research Methods
    Research Designs
    A Final Word About Research

LEARNING OBJECTIVES

After reading Chapter 1, you should be able to:
- Discuss the realities of marriage and family life today
- Discuss whether marriage and the family in America are in decline
- Summarize why many marriages end in divorce
- Discuss how couples can best prepare for marriage
- Describe how families are changing
- Summarize continuity and change in marriage and family trends
- Discuss how one begins to develop a personal set of principles or concepts that will help in understanding family life
- Discuss the variety of conceptual frameworks in family science
- Discuss how research on the family is conducted

PRACTICE TESTS
Key Terms

1. A(n) _____ includes general principles composed of interrelated concepts and hypotheses.
2. The _____ perspective focuses on identifying the foundation for continued growth and change in a family.
3. A description of how family members see their relationships utilizes a(n) _____.
4. _____ is a multidisciplinary field—a profession as well as a social science—that contributes to the understanding of families.
5. Two or more individuals who are committed to one another and who share intimacy, resources, and values constitute a(n) _____.
6. _____ is achieved when a research instrument measures what it is intended to measure.
7. A computerized system containing research articles on families is called a(n) _____.
8. A set of interconnected ideas, concepts, and assumptions, referred to as a(n) _____, helps organize thinking from a particular perspective.
9. _____ is used in research to compare findings from two data-collecting methods to increase validity.
10. _____ are national family databases available to students and researchers through large libraries.
11. _____ involves the emotional and legal commitment of two people to share emotional and physical intimacy, various tasks, and economic resources.
12. As a result of immigration patterns and social and global trends and policies, the United States is becoming an increasingly _____.
13. A(n) _____ on family life is provided by researchers or therapists.
14. A(n) _____ selected in research studies is more likely to be obtained by utilizing a random selection of families.
15. The interconnection of all family members is viewed as a(n) _____.
16. Using family systems theory, a focus on the family or the couple is on the _____.
17. Attempting to avoid change is being _____.
18. Providing _____ usually results in minimizing change and keeping things the same.
19. _____ involves a set of principles and concepts applicable to all types of systems.
20. Being open to growth and change is to be _____.
21. Focusing on the entire system being more than the sum of its parts is a belief in the concept of _____.
22. Interconnected systems, arranged within a hierarchy with each system being larger than the one before, is referred to as _____.
23. Viewing the study of the relationship of humans in a biological system is the _____.
24. Family systems that are accessible to growth and change are _____.
25. A focus on the individual family members when using family systems theory is to focus on the _____.
26. An approach that views all family members as having an impact on everyone else in the family is the _____.

27. _____ decrease the interconnectedness in systems by pushing system elements away from one another.
28. _____ increases the likelihood of effecting change.
29. Family systems that work to maintain the status quo are _____.
30. Behaviors that result in increasing interconnectedness in systems are _____.
31. When _____ is present, one part is automatically affected if another part is changed.

Multiple Choice

1. Approximately what percentage of the United States population marries at least once?
    a. 40
    b. 55
    c. 70
    d. 90

2. More than ____ percent of all recent marriages in the United States are likely to end in divorce.
    a. 25
    b. 40
    c. 50
    d. 65

3. Which of the following persons is LEAST LIKELY to remarry after divorce?
    a. a noncustodial father
    b. a woman with no children
    c. a custodial father
    d. a woman with three children

4. From a family systems theory perspective, when a child of a single parent constantly gets in trouble at school:
    a. the child is the problem
    b. the teacher is the problem
    c. everybody in the family (including the noncustodial parent) is the problem
    d. Family systems theory does not apply, since school problems are outside of the family's boundaries.

5. Which is NOT typically found in currently used definitions of the family?
    a. two or more people
    b. commitment of its members
    c. procreating/having children
    d. shared resources

6. Which statistic regarding marriages and families had the highest rate of *increase* between 1960 and 1990?
    a. percentage of childbirths outside of marriage
    b. percentage of teenage mothers who are unmarried
    c. divorced individuals per 1,000 married individuals
    d. percentage of adult life spent with spouse and children

7. Which of the following is NOT an example of positive communication?
    a. sarcasm
    b. humor
    c. avoiding verbal conflict
    d. a and c

8. Which American ethnic group has the highest percentage of single parents?
   a. white
   b. Latino
   c. African American
   d. Asian American

9. The average number of children per family in the United States currently is:
   a. 1.7
   b. 2.2
   c. 2.7
   d. 3.2

10. Currently, about _____ percent of all U.S. families are stepfamilies.
    a. 12
    b. 20
    c. 35
    d. 44

11. Which conceptual framework studies families as an interconnected group or system?
    a. social interaction
    b. symbolic interaction
    c. feminist
    d. family systems

12. According to the _____ conceptual framework, family interaction is understood in the context of how the family members perceive their situation.
    a. family systems
    b. social interaction
    c. symbolic interaction
    d. feminist

13. A research instrument which measures what it intends to measure is considered:
    a. biased
    b. valid
    c. reliable
    d. nomothetic

14. The _____ is likely the most commonly used method of studying families.
    a. questionnaire
    b. interview
    c. case study
    d. observation

15. Of those who get divorced, about _____ percent eventually remarry.
    a. 75
    b. 60
    c. 40
    d. 30

True/False

1. Most social scientists agree that the social institution of the family is in serious danger of totally disintegrating.

2. Although the number of single-parent families increased in the 1970s, the number has leveled off since the late 1980s.

3. Both parents work in more than 50 percent of U.S. families.

4. The median age for first marriage has been on the increase over the past three decades for men but not for women.

5. The rate of cohabitation has increased dramatically among *both* previously unmarried and divorced individuals since the 1960s.

6. The divorce rate, although it increased during the 1960s and 1970s, has stabilized in the 1990s.

7. Following divorce, women are likely to remarry more quickly and more frequently than are men.

8. Truly strong families generally exhibit to some degree each of the six strength clusters identified by researchers.

9. Most family professionals utilize an eclectic approach rather than a single conceptual framework to help them understand what is going on in a family.

Short Answer

1. What are three reasons for the large numbers of divorces and unhappy marriages in our society?

2. List three advantages of feminism for women and three advantages for men.

3. Name five of the characteristics common to marriages, according to Broderick.

4. What accounts for the family as possibly being the most difficult social institution to research?

5. Identify and describe three types of research studies that include time as a consideration.

Name _____   Chapter 1

PERSONAL INVOLVEMENT ASSESSMENT—
ATTITUDES TOWARD MARRIAGE, DIVORCE, AND UNMARRIED MOTHERHOOD

Inarguably, Americans hold many different views about marriage, divorce, and unmarried motherhood. What accounts for the differences—whether we are female or male? poor or wealthy? black, Latino, or white? part of an intact or a single-parent family?

Katherine Trent and Scott South checked for these and other possible determinants, using data from the 1987–88 National Survey of Families and Households (NSFH), which sampled more than 13,000 adults. In one part of the study, respondents answered the five questions below about their level of approval of various behaviors related to marriage, divorce, and parenthood. Their responses were tallied according to gender, race, whether their mother had worked, and whether they had ever lived with their father.

Assessment. Indicate how you view the behaviors and statements below by circling the response that best fits your attitude. Then compare your views with those of the NSFH respondents.

1. Women who have a child without getting married.   Approve   Disapprove

2. A couple with an unhappy marriage getting a divorce if their youngest child is under 5.   Approve   Disapprove

3. It's better for a person to get married than to go through life being single.   Agree   Disagree

4. Marriage is a lifetime relationship and should never be ended except under extreme circumstances.   Agree   Disagree

5. Children have fewer problems with two natural parents than with one natural parent and one stepparent.   Agree   Disagree

---

Source of this section is Katherine Trent and Scott J. South, "Sociodemographic Status, Parental Background, Childhood Family Structure, and Attitudes Toward Family Formation," *Journal of Marriage and the Family* 54 (May 1992): 427–439.

Survey Results. Results given are percentage *agreeing* or *disapproving*.

	1. Nonmar. childbear. (% Disapp.)	2. Divorce with kids (% Disapp.)	3. Better to marry (% Agree)	4. Marriage for life (% Agree)	5. Natural parents (% Disagree)
Sex					
Female	58.2	28.3	41.1	72.4	43.1
Male	60.0	40.9	54.8	77.6	54.0
Race					
Black	49.6	39.3	43.3	72.1	45.6
Hispanic	51.0	48.5	62.7	79.5	57.9
White	60.8	32.5	46.8	74.8	47.7
Mother worked:					
Yes	53.0	30.1	40.2	71.7	42.3
No	64.6	38.1	54.2	77.7	53.6
Ever lived with father:					
Yes	59.7	34.3	47.9	75.1	48.8
No	44.9	32.4	39.1	69.7	35.9

Discussion. Indicate how your views compared with those found in the survey.

Name _____   Chapter 1

KNOWLEDGE IN ACTION—
FAMILY SCIENCE RESEARCH

Chapter 1 presents information in Box 1.5 on reference books, journals, and indexes, as well as computed databases, typically available in college and university libraries. These include the *International Bibliography of Research in Marriage and the Family* and the *Inventory of Marriage and Family Literature,* found in volumes as well as on databases. Both the *DIALOGUE* and *BIBLIOGRAPHIC RETRIEVAL SYSTEMS (BRS)* are national databases that can be used to locate research journals and books.

Project. Visit your school library and spend some time locating the reference volumes as well as databases. Select one specific topic—e.g., divorce, family policy, stepfamilies, family systems framework—and conduct a search through the library's reference systems and databases using this topic. Then complete the following items.

1. Topic:
2.
   | *Reference/Database* | *Number of Sources Found* |

   a.

   b.

   c.

   d.

   e.

ANSWER KEY

Key Terms

1. theory
2. family strengths
3. insider perspective
4. Family science
5. family
6. Validity
7. family database
8. conceptual framework
9. Cross-validation
10. DIALOGUE and Bibliographic Retrieval Systems (BRS)
11. Marriage
12. multicultural society
13. outsider perspective
14. representative sample
15. family system
16. suprasystem
17. morphostatic
18. negative feedback
19. General systems theory
20. morphogenic
21. wholeness
22. boundaries
23. ecological approach
24. open system
25. subsystem
26. family systems framework
27. Centrifugal interactions
28. Positive feedback
29. closed system
30. centripetal interactions
31. interdependence on parts

Multiple Choice

1. d
2. c
3. d
4. c
5. c
6. a
7. d
8. c
9. a
10. b
11. d
12. c
13. b
14. a
15. a

True/False

1. F
2. F
3. F
4. F
5. T
6. T
7. F
8. F
9. T

Suggested Responses to Short Answer Questions

1. 1) People entering marriage with unrealistic expectations; 2) marrying the wrong person for the wrong reasons; 3) the difficult nature of marriage, even if the partner is chosen wisely; 4) decline in intimacy and marital quality over a period of time; 5) inability of couples to handle major stressors in married life.

2. Three advantages of feminism for women are providing women an identity separate from their family roles when working outside the home, independent economic security, and an opportunity to develop their full potential. Advantages for men are reducing pressure of being solely responsible for supporting their family, participating in their children's development, and having the opportunity to develop their full potential.

3. Marriage is 1) a demographic event; 2) the joining of two family and social networks; 3) a legal contract; 4) an economic union; 5) the most common form of adult cohabitation; 6) the context of most human sexual activity; 7) a reproductive unit; 8) a unit that socializes children; and 9) an opportunity to develop an intimate, sharing relationship.

4. Families tend to be closed to outsiders and to present as positive an image to outsiders as they can. Family realities can be difficult for researchers to learn about.

5. 1) Longitudinal studies—interviewing and observing of families over an extended period of time; 2) cross-sectional studies—studying and contrasting families at various stages of the family life cycle; 3) cross-sectional cohort studies—studying various families each at different stages of the family life cycle.

CHAPTER 2

CULTURAL DIVERSITY: FAMILY STRENGTHS AND CHALLENGES

CHAPTER OUTLINE

The Nature of Cultural Diversity
    A Changing Picture: Demographic Trends in the United States
    The Mythology of Race
    Kin Relationships Across Cultures: Concepts and Terms

Family Strengths, Stereotypes, and Challenges in Various Ethnic and Cultural Groups
    Strengths of White Families
    Strengths of African American Families
    Strengths of Latino Families
    Strengths of Asian American Families
    Strengths of Native American Families

Challenges for Ethnic Families
    Marriage Outside the Group
    Black-White Marriages
    Assimilation, Acculturation, or Segregation
    Relationships Between Men and Women
    Relationships Between Parents and Children

Issues in Cross-Cultural Family Studies
    Ethnocentrism
    Racism
    Appreciating Diversity

LEARNING OBJECTIVES

After reading Chapter 2, you should be able to:
- Describe how the image of a rainbow of ethnic diversity is a useful analogy among those who celebrate the value and benefits of our multicolored and multicultured nation
- Compare and contrast how Latino, African American, Native American, Asian American, and white families structure their marital and sexual relationships
- Summarize the mythology of race
- Explain the three kinship groupings
- Discuss the proposition that strong families across the country and around the world share three major clusters of qualities: cohesion, flexibility, and communication
- Explain why there is no such thing as a "typical" or "stereotypical" white, African American, or Latino family
- Explain the term *ethnocentrism* and how it is related to *racism*
- Summarize the principles for appreciating diversity
- Discuss how intercultural marriage can create problems in a family and how these problems can be overcome

PRACTICE TESTS

Key Terms

1. Cultural or social groups with distinctness apart from the dominant culture but living within it are _____.
2. A kin group in which norms are such that both the females and the males are respected and considered is a(n) _____.
3. Newly married couples living with or near the husband's kin are in a(n) _____.
4. Societies in which lineage goes through males are _____.
5. A(n) _____ has less power than the dominant group and always experiences some form of prejudice and discrimination.
6. The smallest kinship unit that is part of a conjugal family system is the _____.
7. A relatively transitory system formed through marriage is the _____.
8. _____ involves an aversion to homosexuality.
9. A kin group in which females exercise authority is a(n) _____.
10. Adopting the norms and values of the new culture is _____.
11. A man with more than one wife practices _____.
12. The physical characteristics of a specific group of people are referred to as _____, although not in a scientific way.
13. The judging of other cultures using the standards of one's own culture is _____.
14. Kinship groups comprised of individuals unrelated by legal or blood relationships but having close ties that resemble kinship ties are referred to as _____ groups.
15. _____ indicates lines of descent.
16. A woman with more than one husband practices _____.
17. The _____ focuses on similarities among cultures.
18. _____ refers to the geographic origins of a culture's minorities.
19. Newly married couples living independently and separately from either spouse's kin group are in a(n) _____.
20. A(n) _____ involves a marriage between one individual and two or more spouses.
21. The intertwining of cultural traits and values of an ethnic group with those of the dominant culture is _____.
22. _____ governs behavior, norms, and roles among individuals related to one another.
23. Societies which use a "family tree" lineage are of _____.
24. A kin group in which males exercise authority is a(n) _____.
25. A(n) _____ is comprised of two or more nuclear families related by blood ties.
26. _____ occurs when an ethnic group is either forced into isolation or imposes self-isolation.
27. A marriage having one husband and one wife is known as a(n) _____ union.
28. _____, which benefits the group in power, focuses on differences rather than similarities between the minority group and the dominant group and often results in conflict.
29. A(n) _____ is comprised of families connected by blood ties more than by marriage ties.

30. A(n) _____ perspective focuses on similarities and differences among cultures.
31. Chinese American is an example of a(n) _____.
32. Societies in which lineage goes through females are _____.
33. The _____ focuses on differences among cultures.
34. Newly married couples living with or near the wife's kin are in a(n) _____.

Multiple Choice

1. Which term is used to refer to the geographic origins of the minorities of a particular country or culture?
   a. cultural identity
   b. ethnicity
   c. race
   d. co-culture

2. The largest ethnic minority group in the United States is:
   a. African Americans
   b. Asian Americans
   c. Latinos
   d. Native Americans

3. The fastest-growing minority group in the United States is:
   a. Latinos
   b. African Americans
   c. Asian Americans
   d. gay and lesbian couples

4. Which is NOT a usual characteristic distinguishing an ethnic group?
   a. religious views
   b. language
   c. race
   d. physical characteristics

5. In which type of society is descent traced through females?
   a. matrilineal
   b. matriarchal
   c. matrilocal
   d. bilateral

6. Which type of norms pertain to newly married couples establishing a separate, autonomous residence, apart from either partner's kin group?
   a. bilateral
   b. pseudo-kin
   c. equalitarian
   d. neolocal

7. Research conducted by Gary and associates of strong African American families found that their strengths exhibited differences along two variables from those of healthy white families, with more importance placed on _____ in African American families.
   a. work and health
   b. religious values and kinship ties
   c. education and religious values
   d. kinship ties and health

8. Which ethnic group places the well-being of the entire family system over individual goals?
   a. African Americans
   b. Latinos
   c. Native Americans
   d. Asian Americans

9. Which is a common family problem identified in the text as occurring in many ethnic groups?
   a. family roles
   b. religious conflict
   c. work-family conflicts
   d. conflicts between generations

10. Which ethnic group places special importance on its identification with living in harmony with nature, a spiritual orientation to life, and traditional religious practices?
    a. African Americans
    b. Latinos
    c. Native Americans
    d. Asian Americans

11. Discrimination against Asian Americans is most likely fueled by:
    a. fear of competition
    b. religious prejudice
    c. economic envy
    d. all of the above

12. Many therapists and gays believe intense homophobia may be a result of:
    a. low self-esteem
    b. discomfort with one's sexuality
    c. past homosexual experiences
    d. negative encounters with gays

13. To Kinsey's study of sexual behavior, _____ of men and _____ of women reported being sexually oriented exclusively to members of their own sex.
    a. 10 percent; 10 percent
    b. 10 percent; 6 percent
    c. 6 percent; 3 percent
    d. 4 percent; 2 percent

14. Social shame, rather than physical punishment, is a common tool for disciplining children among:
    a. African Americans
    b. Latinos
    c. Native Americans
    d. Asian Americans

15. The most critical criterion for identifying an individual's ethnic group is his or her:
    a. language
    b. religion
    c. self-perception
    d. ancestry

True/False

1. The term *race* is based on scientific classification.

2. Latino families today tend to be characterized by male dominance and authoritarian fathering.

3. Strong family traditions are more likely to develop in consanguineal rather than conjugal family systems.

4. Family patterns tend to operate smoothly in groups in which plural marriages are the custom.

5. The criterion of age always supersedes that of gender in matriarchal and patriarchal kin groups.
6. The rate of child mistreatment among lower-income African Americans is higher than that for lower-income whites.
7. Younger Puerto Ricans studied by Rogler and Cooney (1984) tended to have developed a stronger ethnic identity than their parents had.
8. Intercultural couples are somewhat more likely than same-culture couples to divorce.
9. Relative number of people in a group is not what determines whether it is a minority or majority group.
10. Asian Americans face the same level of discrimination in the workplace as African Americans.

Short Answer

1. Describe how the United States is more like a salad bowl than a melting pot.

2. Why is there some ambiguity about referring to Jews as an ethnic group?

3. Identify and briefly describe the three major clusters of qualities found in strong families across ethnic identification or country of origin.

4. Define "pseudo-kin" and give two examples.

5. Give three reasons why social and behavioral science research focuses mainly on whites.

Name _____   Chapter 2

PERSONAL INVOLVEMENT ASSESSMENT—STEREOTYPING

Stereotypes, or overgeneralizations about a whole category or group of people, usually present distorted images of both the group and its individual members. Stereotypes can be used to rationalize prejudice (an attitude) and to justify discrimination (behavior). People typically use stereotypes for groups other than the ones to which they belong or with which they identify, such as those based on race/ethnicity, religion, and sexual preference.

What are some commonly used stereotypes pertaining to the five groups discussed in the text as well as to whites—the dominant group in American society? List a few stereotypes that you are aware of for each of the groups, indicating your level of agreement with each (SA = Strongly Agree, A = Agree, N = Neutral/Don't Know, D = Disagree, SD = Strongly Disagree). Discuss what you believe are the fallacies of each stereotype, based on the material presented in the chapter.

African American Families

Stereotypes	Agreement	Discussion

Latino Families

Stereotypes	Agreement	Discussion

Asian American Families

Stereotypes	Agreement	Discussion

Native American Families

Stereotypes	Agreement	Discussion

White Families

Stereotypes	Agreement	Discussion

Name _____   Chapter 2

KNOWLEDGE IN ACTION—
CONDUCTING A LIFE HISTORY

One example of what life has been like for a graduate student who has experienced cultural conflict is related in Chapter 2 in the text in Box 2.4. Told by Julie Palacio about her own life, the excerpt from her unpublished manuscript is moving in relating how conflict occurred for her when her career goals did not coincide with what her family of origin thought she should be doing.

As is brought out in Chapter 2, individuals can experience conflict with family members of other generations as well as conflict between traditional values and the values of the dominant group in society.

Project. For this project, conduct an interview with another student, someone with a different ethnic/cultural heritage or sexual orientation from your own. Prepare some questions ahead of time that have to do with the individual's upbringing, family values and norms, attitudes toward the dominant group in society, views on racism/ethnocentrism in American society, intercultural marriage, assimilation, and other topics covered in this chapter. Following the interview, discuss the individual's responses and compare/contrast them with your upbringing, values, etc.

Person Interviewed:

   Name:

   Age:

   Cultural heritage/Sexual orientation:

   Major:

   Other particulars:

Questions asked:

Summary of responses:

Discussion:

ANSWER KEY

Key Terms

1. co-cultures
2. equalitarian group
3. patrilocal society
4. patrilineal
5. minority group
6. nuclear family
7. conjugal family system
8. Homophobia
9. matriarchal group
10. assimilation
11. polygamy
12. race
13. ethnocentrism
14. pseudo-kin
15. Lineage
16. polyandry
17. emic perspective
18. Ethnic identity
19. neolocal society
20. plural marriage
21. acculturation
22. Kinship
23. bilateral descent
24. patriarchal group
25. extended family
26. Segregation
27. monogamous
28. Racism
29. consanguineal system
30. cross-cultural family study
31. cultural identity
32. matrilineal
33. etic perspective
34. matrilocal society

Multiple Choice

1. b
2. a
3. c
4. c
5. a
6. d
7. b
8. b
9. d
10. c
11. b
12. b
13. d
14. c
15. c

True/False

1. F
2. F
3. T
4. T
5. F
6. F
7. F
8. T
9. T
10. F

Suggested Responses to Short Answer Questions

1. The United States has many diverse cultural groups, each of which has retained many of its distinctive "flavors," or values, norms, traditions, etc. A melting pot would be a society in which the distinct cultures have lost their uniqueness and blended into one society.

2. 1) Jews as individuals vary widely in their religious views; 2) they speak a wide variety of languages, and many cannot speak Hebrew, the traditional language; 3) they have diverse ancestral backgrounds, especially as many people have converted to Judaism; 4) they have a wide variety of physical characteristics; and 5) they follow different cultural heritages.

3. 1) Cohesion includes commitment to the family and spending quality time sharing activities, feelings, and ideas and enjoying each other's company; 2) flexibility includes the ability to deal with stress and having spiritual beliefs; 3) communication includes focusing on positive communication and on appreciating and having affection for family members.

4. "Pseudo-kin" refers to a group in which unrelated individuals have relationships which resemble those in kinship groups, such as being close and intense.

5. 1) Most researchers come from white middle- or upper-class backgrounds; 2) individuals tend to be more interested in their own group than in other groups and may more readily recognize the relevance of research questions focusing on their own group; 3) many white researchers may question their ability to research people from other cultural backgrounds and to see the world from a minority-group perspective; 4) many often comment that few people from other ethnic groups volunteer to participate in their studies.

CHAPTER 3

UNDERSTANDING RELATIONSHIPS IN MARRIAGE AND FAMILY

CHAPTER OUTLINE

Cohesion, Flexibility, and Communication
    Family Systems Theory
    The Family Strengths Framework
    The Family Development Framework

The Family Circumplex Model: A Tool for Understanding Families
    Cohesion
    Flexibility
    Communication
    The Circumplex Model As a Relationship Map

Movies As Illustrations of Family Circumplex Types
    What About Bob: A Rigidly Connected Family
    Ordinary People: A Rigidly Disengaged Family
    Shoot the Moon: A Chaotically Disengaged Family

Dynamic Change in Family Relationships
    Changes in Early Marriage
    Family Cohesion Across the Family Life Cycle
    Family Flexibility Across the Family Life Cycle

LEARNING OBJECTIVES

After reading Chapter 3, you should be able to:
- Discuss the Family Circumplex Model and its three central dimensions and explain how it is related to the Family Strengths Model
- Discuss the Family Circumplex Model as a relationship map
- Using the concept of dynamic balance of cohesion and flexibility, describe couples and families who function best and worst across the life cycle
- Compare balanced and unbalanced types of families
- Explain how the Family Circumplex Model is relevant for describing a variety of families with different ethnic and cultural backgrounds
- Define *family cohesion* and explain the importance of a balance between separateness and togetherness
- Define *family flexibility* and explain the importance of a balance between stability and change
- Trace how the relationship of a couple changes in cohesiveness and flexibility from courtship through five years of marriage
- Discuss family cohesion and flexibility across the family life cycle
- Explain how the Circumplex Model can be used to help premarital couples strengthen their relationship

PRACTICE TESTS

Key Terms

1. The dimension of the Family Circumplex Model having to do with togetherness is _____.
2. _____—the ability to change—is the second dimension represented graphically in the Family Circumplex Model.
3. The dimension that facilitates a family's movement between the extremes of the cohesion and flexibility dimensions of the Family Circumplex Model is _____.
4. Families that are labeled flexibly connected, flexibly cohesive, structurally connected, or structurally cohesive are _____ on the Circumplex Model.
5. _____ are extreme on one dimension of the Circumplex Model but balanced on the other dimensions.
6. _____ occurs when an individual believes that everything done by another person reflects on himself or herself.
7. Openness to growth and change involves _____.
8. _____ increases the likelihood of effecting change.
9. _____ are likely to be found at the extremes of the dimensions using the Family Circumplex Model.
10. The amount of change that occurs *within* any given family system is _____.
11. Behaviors that result in increasing interconnectedness in systems are _____.
12. The _____ is used to locate, map, and understand family relationships.
13. _____ involves change from one system to another system type.
14. Attempting to avoid change involves _____.
15. _____ lessens the interconnectedness in systems by pushing system elements away from one another.

Multiple Choice

1. David Reiss's concept of closure is similar to the _____ dimension of the Family Circumplex Model.
    a. cohesion
    b. flexibility
    c. communication
    d. problem solving

2. A family's ability to cope with stress and crisis will be most influenced by its:
    a. centripetal forces
    b. centrifugal forces
    c. flexibility
    d. cohesion

3. According to the Family Circumplex Model, too much togetherness can lead to:
    a. disengagement
    b. dependence
    c. rigidity
    d. enmeshment

4. _____ can become problematic for a couple because it tends to stifle individuality.
   a. Flexibility
   b. Engagement
   c. Enmeshment
   d. Connectedness

5. Which type of family is characterized by the premise that "nothing is constant in life but change"?
   a. chaotic
   b. flexible
   c. structured
   d. rigid

6. The _____ type of family is characterized by controlled emotions, strictly defined roles, and strict but unspoken rules about expression of feelings.
   a. rigidly enmeshed
   b. rigidly disengaged
   c. chaotically disengaged
   d. chaotically enmeshed

7. Which type of relationship is found in a couple who has been married for one year, the "honeymoon effect" has worn off, and their togetherness is more balanced than earlier in their marriage?
   a. structurally enmeshed
   b. structurally cohesive
   c. flexibly disengaged
   d. rigidly connected

8. This same couple, now having been together for five years since starting dating and having a year-old baby and their life together has been stabilized, are functioning as a _____ family.
   a. structurally enmeshed
   b. structurally cohesive
   c. flexibly disengaged
   d. rigidly connected

9. A study of family cohesion among 1,000 non-problem families, conducted by Olson and his colleagues, found that the highest percentage of young couples without children felt _____.
   a. cohesive
   b. connected
   c. engaged
   d. enmeshed

10. Among non-problem families with teenagers, the highest percentage of couples felt _____, according to Olson and his colleagues.
    a. cohesive
    b. connected
    c. engaged
    d. enmeshed

11. Olson and his colleagues also found that young couples without children were more likely to be _____ than _____.
    a. structured; flexible
    b. flexible; structured
    c. engaged; enmeshed
    d. enmeshed; flexible

12. The _____ family is exemplified by a wife's returning to work after several years staying at home, with the husband now helping out around the house and with the children pitching in as well.
    a. structurally enmeshed
    b. flexibly disengaged
    c. flexibly connected
    d. structurally connected

13. Economic stress affecting a family is an example of:
    a. centrifugal force
    b. chaotic cohesiveness
    c. centripetal force
    d. family coordination

14. A family therapist likely would advise a couple that is too _____ to develop separate interests and spend more time apart.
    a. disengaged
    b. cohesive
    c. connected
    d. enmeshed

15. The rigidly enmeshed family is characterized by:
    a. strict enforcement of family rules by the father, who is the center of the family
    b. an outwardly pleasant but passively controlling structure
    c. a lack of consistency in rules and roles
    d. love-hate relationships bound by mutual dependence

True/False

1. According to the Family Circumplex Model, couples and families who appear to function best during the life cycle seem to measure stronger on the togetherness dimension than on the separateness dimension.

2. Families do change the kind of system they have (under the Family Circumplex Model) as changes occur in the family life cycle.

3. There tends to be a linear relationship between both cohesion and flexibility and family functioning, according to the Family Circumplex Model.

4. Disengaged relationships are those characterized by high levels of independence.

5. Most families tend to work to maintain the status quo rather than to effect change.

6. Relationships that change too much over time can become unpredictable and chaotic.

7. Olson and his colleagues found that in 1,000 non-problem families, adolescents saw their families as significantly higher in cohesion than did their parents.

8. Research findings do NOT offer strong support for the notion that balanced families are more functional than unbalanced families.

9. Balanced families do NOT function at extreme levels of cohesion or flexibility.

10. The extreme low level of cohesion is referred to as disengagement.

Short Answer

1. Identify and briefly describe the three dimensions of the Family Circumplex Model.

2. List the 16 types of family relationships clustered by type of family system, as found in the relationship map.

3. What is meant by the Family Circumplex Model's being a "dynamic" model?

4. What problems commonly arise in enmeshed relationships?

5. What are the four groups of families examined by Clarke in studying families with severe problems?

Name _____   Chapter 3

PERSONAL INVOLVEMENT ASSESSMENT—
FAMILIES CIRCUMPLEX MODEL

Chapter 3 provides information on the Family Circumplex Model developed by Olson and Sprenkle (1989). For this assessment, which is also found in the Activities section at the end of Chapter 3, you are to determine where your own family fits in the model. Select either Option 1 or Option 2.

Option 1. Use the Family Circumplex Scales (Table 3.5 in the text, page 108) to describe your family of origin. Select a time period when you were all together (e.g., when you were in high school). Make a list of the people you are including in your family. Then do the following:

a. Review the six categories shown in the scales (Table 3.5 in the text) for assessing cohesion, flexibility, and communication.

b. On a separate piece of paper, rate your family on a scale of 1–8 for each of the three dimensions.

c. To obtain *a total score for each category,* review the scores and select the number that represents the best average score. Record the score below.

Family Cohesion   **Family Flexibility**   **Family Communication**

Score: _____   Score: _____   Score: _____

Level: _____   Level: _____   Level: _____

d. Now plot the scores for cohesion and flexibility onto the Family Circumplex Model and identify the *type of family system* in which you grew up.

e. After plotting your scores onto the model, consider the following questions:

- What is/was it like to live in your type of family (e.g., flexibly connected, rigidly enmeshed, etc.)?

- In what ways related to cohesion and flexibility is/was your family satisfying and in what ways is/was it frustrating?

- How did you family change on cohesion and flexibility as you were growing up?

- In what ways did communication affect your family's dynamics?

Option 2. If you are dating someone, are engaged, or are married, both you and your partner should answer the questions on the Family Circumplex Scales twice: first in terms of your families of origin (same as Option 1) and second, in terms of your couple relationship. Compare your partner's descriptions with yours about your couple relationship, and discuss the similarities and differences. Then compare each of your families of origin with your couple relationship.

Name _____   Chapter 3

KNOWLEDGE IN ACTION—
FAMILIES IN THE MEDIA

Chapter 3 of the text provides examples of three different Family Circumplex types as reflected in films. These include the family in *What About Bob* as an example of a rigidly connected family, the family in *Ordinary People* as rigidly disengaged, and the family in *Shoot the Moon* as chaotically disengaged.

Project. For this assignment, select three different television programs or films you have seen, each exemplifying a family of a different Family Circumplex type. You may choose the types used as examples in Chapter 3 or any of the other Family Circumplex types described in the chapter, e.g., flexibly disengaged, structurally cohesive, etc. As was done in the chapter, describe how the family in each film or television program you have selected fits the particular Family Circumplex type.

1. Title (of film or television program):
   Family Circumplex type:
   Description (of how the family illustrates the Family Circumplex type):

2. Title:
   Family Circumplex type:
   Description:

3. Title:
   Family Circumplex type:
   Description:

ANSWER KEY

Key Terms

1. cohesion
2. Flexibility
3. communication
4. Balanced families
5. Mid-range families
6. Personification
7. morphogenic processes
8. Positive feedback
9. Unbalanced families
10. first order change
11. centripetal interaction
12. Family Circumplex Model
13. Second order change
14. morphostatic processes
15. Centrifugal interaction

Multiple Choice

1. b
2. c
3. d
4. c
5. a
6. b
7. b
8. d
9. a
10. b
11. b
12. b
13. a
14. d
15. a

True/False

1. F
2. T
3. F
4. T
5. T
6. T
7. F
8. F
9. F
10. T

Suggested Responses to Short Answer Questions

1. 1) Cohesion—togetherness, 2) flexibility—ability to change, 3) communication—the dimension that helps facilitate a family's movement between the extremes of cohesion and flexibility.

2. Balanced families: flexibly connected, flexibly cohesive, structurally connected, structurally cohesive; Mid-range families: flexibly disengaged, flexibly enmeshed, structurally disengaged, structurally enmeshed; Unbalanced families: chaotically disengaged, chaotically enmeshed, rigidly disengaged, rigidly enmeshed.

3. It assumes that relationships change over time and that couples and families will change over the family life cycle.

4. The couple can get on each other's nerves, become jealous and controlling, and stifle each other's individual development.

5. Families with a neurotic member, families with a schizophrenic member, families who had sought therapy, and families who had not sought therapy.

CHAPTER 4

FRIENDSHIP, LOVE, AND INTIMACY

CHAPTER OUTLINE

Friends Versus Lovers
    The Fabric of Friendship
    The Tapestry of Love
    Contrasting Friends and Lovers
    The Love Triangle
    Three Perspectives on Love

Exploring Intimacy: From Experience to Relationship
    Intimacy Versus Isolation
    Intimacy and Communication
    Intimate Experiences Versus an Intimate Relationship
    The Paradox of Marriage and Intimacy

Developing Intimacy
    Traits of Intimate and Nonintimate Relationships
    Ten Essential Couple Relationship Strengths

Intimacy Games
    Constructive Intimacy Games
    Destructive Intimacy Games
    Limiting Destructive Games

LEARNING OBJECTIVES

After reading Chapter 4, you should be able to:
- Discuss the difference between love and friendship
- Define *intimacy*
- Explain how communication enhances intimacy
- Discuss the paradox of marriage and intimacy
- Explain the difference between intimate and nonintimate relationships
- Understand what a constructive intimacy game is
- Know how to limit destructive intimacy games

PRACTICE TESTS

Key Terms

1. The _____, including fascination, exclusiveness, and sexual desire, is found in romantic relationships but not in friendships.
2. Giving the utmost and being an advocate for one's partner are characteristics of the _____.
3. Love containing all three dimensions—commitment, intimacy, and passion—is _____.
4. _____ occurs with the presence of intimacy, but without passion or commitment.
5. When one develops a cognitive attachment to another that develops slowly at the beginning and increases as the relationship becomes increasingly positive, one forms a(n) _____ to the other individual.
6. A love relationship marked only by passion is _____.
7. Couples together a long time who are committed and intimate, but who no longer experience passion, are likely to share _____.
8. _____ can be useful for couples in assessing their level of intimacy and satisfaction with their marriage.
9. Although sometimes positive, _____ usually are destructive because they involve an individual's concealing what he or she wants and attempting to manipulate her or his partner to get it.
10. Lack of commitment, intimacy, or passion is indicative of a state of _____.
11. _____ involves high levels of closeness marked by sharing of feelings, emotional support, and self-disclosure.
12. Commitment without passion or intimacy is likely _____.
13. Lacking in commitment, _____ involves both intimacy and passion.
14. Commitment based on passion can occur in _____, and this is likely the case before true intimacy has had time to develop.
15. _____, intensity of feelings usually expressed by physiological arousal and affection, is one dimension of love.
16. Having a(n) _____ involves the sharing of close experiences with someone in several ways over a period of time.
17. Closeness shared with someone else in a single situation can be described as a(n) _____.
18. In contrast to a relationship based on cooperativeness, a(n) _____ involves a competitive relationship with one person winning and the other losing.

Multiple Choice

1. Which intimacy game has the potential for improving a relationship in both the short run and the long run?
    a. Zero Sum
    b. Giving Compliments
    c. I Don't Care; You Decide
    d. The Ties That Bind

2. The works of _____ focused mainly on psychosexual development.
    a. Freud
    b. Fromm
    c. Erikson
    d. Sternberg

3. Who wrote about love as being distinguished from an *addicted* type of infatuation?
   a. Fromm
   b. Peele
   c. Dobson
   d. Freud

4. Which was *not* presented as a useful technique for limiting destructive intimacy games?
   a. making rules implicit
   b. naming the game
   c. unveiling game strategies
   d. identifying disguised objectives

5. According to Sternberg, _____ occurs when an individual is committed based on passion but has not yet developed genuine intimacy.
   a. companionate love
   b. romantic love
   c. fatuous love
   d. infatuation

6. Erikson maintains that the young adult's challenge is to develop _____ or risk _____.
   a. independence; dependence
   b. high self-esteem; low self-esteem
   c. affiliation; loneliness
   d. intimacy; isolation

7. Which of the following pertains to a couple's holding expectations that their sharing of intimacy will continue over time?
   a. intimate experience
   b. intimate relationship
   c. idealization
   d. caring

8. According to research conducted by Fowers and Olson with more than 5,000 married couples, _____ was the area of highest agreement in happily married couples.
   a. communication
   b. financial management
   c. personality issues
   d. religious orientation

9. The area showing the greatest difference between happily and unhappily married couples was:
   a. conflict resolution
   b. personality issues
   c. sexual relations
   d. financial management

10. To Fowers and Olson, _____ is (are) an emotional thermometer of the quality of a couple's relationship.
    a. conflict resolution
    b. communication
    c. sexual relations
    d. equalitarian roles

11. The most common intimacy game rule is:
    a. withdraw sullenly
    b. name the game
    c. don't directly ask for what you want
    d. overcompliment the other person

12. Which component of Sternberg's love triangle has to do with motivation?
    a. commitment
    b. intimacy
    c. passion

13. Which component of Sternberg's love triangle is characterized by a mature relationship in which most areas are open for discussion and sharing?
    a. commitment
    b. intimacy
    c. passion

14. To what do the authors attribute the prevalence of in-law jokes?
    a. the difficulty parents have letting go of their adult children
    b. the natural hostility individuals feel toward the parents of their spouse
    c. the difficulty people have in expressing their true feelings
    d. the difficulty people have in directly asking for what they want

15. Which constructive intimacy game involves focusing on the positives rather than the negatives and on giving rather than receiving?
    a. giving compliments
    b. asking for what you want directly
    c. encouraging your partner to be honest
    d. self-disclosing

True/False

1. According to Sternberg's love triangle, a couple may experience two or even more types of love over a period of time.
2. To Fromm, "falling in love" is synonymous with "being in love."
3. James Dobson advises the dependent person in the conflicted couple to be tough and pull back from the relationship.
4. Both Freud and Erikson advanced the notion of the psychosexual development of human personality.
5. Family therapists generally express concern that high self-disclosure can result in negative consequences in developing intimacy with others.
6. The truly intimate relationship provides intimate experiences in all areas concurrently.
7. A zero-sum game is one example of a constructive intimacy game.
8. Revealing destructive intimacy games to the participants is generally not a good idea, because it can create further playing of the games.
9. Intimacy games are always destructive.
10. Participants in Davis and Todd's research on friendship and love perceived best friendships as more stable than spouse/love relationships.

Short Answer

1. Identify and briefly define the three dimensions of Sternberg's love triangle.

2. How does Peele view a mature love relationship as different from an addicted love relationship?

3. Briefly describe the paradox of marriage and intimacy.

4. Describe two pitfalls of the two intimacy games "I Don't Care; You Decide" and "The Ties That Bind."

5. What are three things that can be done to limit destructive intimacy games?

6. Identify the two broad categories and their corresponding characteristics found by Davis and Todd to be unique to romantic relationships.

Name _____   Chapter 4

PERSONAL INVOLVEMENT ASSESSMENT—
THE CLOSER YOU GET, THE FASTER I RUN

Ira Wolfman writes of something to which many people can relate: fear of intimacy. In fact, he never leaves home without his "Intimacy Allergy" card. He's a self-admitted "Get close—get away!" guy who has many feelings emerge when faced with intimacy in relationships—for example, nervousness, fear, anger, and craziness. Even though he considers himself to be warm, affectionate, intelligent, and caring, if faced with the possibility that a relationship will become close, he forgets these characteristics when he starts thinking of "marr. . . —you know, the m-word."

Mr. Wolfman, in speaking with Elaine Hatfield of the University of Hawaii at Manoa, learned that his fears of intimacy matched many of the findings of Professor Hatfield's research and that his fears are shared by many—by women perhaps only slightly less than by men.

What fears do you have about intimacy in relationships? Think about any fears you have about getting close, being intimate. Write down five of them. If you do not have any such fears, write down ones you believe are frequently felt by others you know.

1.

2.

3.

4.

5.

Source for this section is Ira Wolfman, "The Closer You Get, the Faster I Run," *Ms.*, September 1985, 934–935, 112.

Read these over and write down what it is that you (or others) appear to fear.

Now, read over the six fears that Mr. Wolfman described.
1. Loving means risking hurt, risking loss, risking abandonment.
2. Oh, God! You'll find out who I really am!
3. Making choices means forsaking choices.
4. You're going to use it against me, aren't you?
5. You'll smother me . . . and I'll hate it.
6. You'll smother me . . . and I'll love it.

Next, write how you relate to these fears.

According to Hatfield, both men and women need to combine the classically feminine need for connection with the classically male need for independence. Presently, therapists utilize various techniques in teaching couples how to achieve greater intimacy, including (1) encouraging people to accept themselves as they are, to recognize their intimates for what they are . . . and let them be, and to express themselves, and (2) teaching people to deal with their intimate's reactions. But Dr. Hatfield cautions: "As long as men were fleeing from intimacy, women could safely pursue them. Now that men are turning around to face them, women may well find themselves taking flight."

Name _____   Chapter 4

KNOWLEDGE IN ACTION—
FRIENDSHIP AND LOVE

"Friendship always benefits; love sometimes injures" (Seneca, first century A.D.). Although this observation was made a long time ago, there may still be some truth to it. Keith E. Davis and Michael J. Todd compared a list of characteristics central to friendship and romantic love with the experiences and expectations of married and single college students and community members. They found that although love and friendship are similar in many ways, there are some differences that can make love relationships more rewarding but also more volatile.

Their profile of friendship included the following characteristics: *enjoyment* of each other's company most of the time; *acceptance* of the other as he or she is without trying to change him or her; *trust* that each will act in the other's best interest; *respect* for each other's good judgment in making life choices; *mutual assistance* in time of need, trouble, or personal distress; *confiding* of experiences and feelings; *understanding* of what is important to each other; and *spontaneity* in feeling free to be oneself in the relationship.

Their profile of romantic love included the same characteristics but in addition *fascination* and preoccupation with each other; *exclusiveness,* which precludes having the same relationship with a third party; *sexual desire* and physical intimacy with each other; *giving the utmost* when the other is in need, sometimes to the point of extreme self-sacrifice; and *being a champion/advocate* of each other's interests and success. They also found *ambivalence, conflict,* and *maintenance* activities in spouse/lover relationships as compared to close friendship relationships.

A major surprise in their data was that 27 percent of their subjects listed a member of the other gender as a best friend (not romantic). Also, 56 percent of the men nominated at least one woman as a close friend, and 44 percent of the women nominated at least one man as a close friend. Thus, even though same-sex friendships predominated, many maintained close friendships with someone of the other gender.

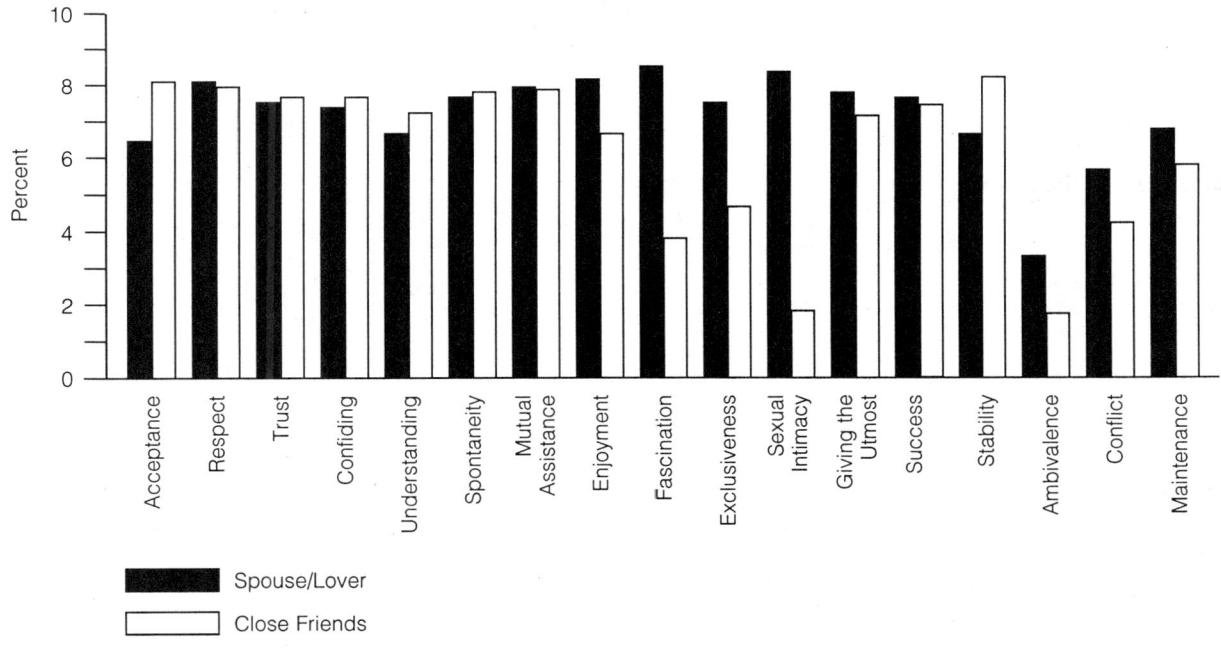

Close friends and lovers compared.

Graph: Keith Davis, "Near and Dear: Friendship and Love Compared," *Psychology Today,* February 1985, pp. 22–28, 30. Reprinted with permission from Psychology Today Magazine. Copyright © 1985 Sussex Publishers, Inc.

Project. Select a sample of male and female students and nonstudents of different ages. Ask each for a list of close friends. Inquire if any of the close friends counts as a "best friend," determine the gender of the close friends, and find out which—if any—is also a spouse, lover, or romantic partner. Then ask for a short description of the relationship with each of the people on the list. Finally, tabulate your data by gender, indicating percentages of close friends who are (a) of the same/opposite gender but not a romantic partner, (b) of the same/opposite gender and considered a best friend, (c) of the same/opposite gender and also a lover/spouse. Also, briefly analyze the characteristics listed for the various types and contrast with the findings portrayed in the graph on the preceding page.

Findings.

Discussion/Implications.

ANSWER KEY

Key Terms

1. passion cluster
2. caring cluster
3. consummate love
4. Liking
5. commitment
6. infatuation
7. companionate love
8. ENRICH
9. intimacy games
10. non-love
11. Intimacy
12. empty love
13. romantic love
14. fatuous love
15. Passion
16. intimate relationship
17. intimate experience
18. zero-sum game

Multiple Choice

1. b
2. a
3. b
4. a
5. c
6. d
7. b
8. d
9. c
10. c
11. c
12. c
13. b
14. a
15. a

True/False

1. T
2. F
3. T
4. F
5. T
6. F
7. F
8. F
9. F
10. T

Suggested Responses to Short Answer Questions

1. 1) Commitment—the cognitive attachment to a partner that develops over time, increasing if the relationship is positive, but disappearing if the relationship fails; 2) intimacy—sharing of feelings and providing of emotional support, involving high levels of self-disclosure; 3) passion—intense feelings and displaying of affection.

2. A mature love relationship involves a couple's valuing themselves, being better people as a result of the relationship, having serious interests outside the relationship, not having the relationship as the totality of their life, not being possessive or jealous of one another, being best friends. An addicted love relationship involves infatuation, highs associated with "the hunt," and continually searching for the high.

3. Although most people marry to achieve intimacy, marriage is only one important source of intimacy and may, in fact, bring about a lessening, or even the elimination, of intimacy for some couples. Although marriage is viewed as the way to achieve happiness, it may also be the source of conflict.

4. "I Don't Care; You Decide": The game-player fails to achieve what she wants because she did not express her true feelings nor actively involve herself in the decision-making process; holding the other person responsible if the decision turns out to be a bad one, thereby causing hard feelings on the part of the other person; having the day/evening ruined for other activities, e.g., making love.

   "The Ties That Bind": Frequently played between parents and adult children, with parents trying to keep their adult children bound to them and their children resenting this, with the consequence of driving them away rather than having them stay close.

5. Identify them, make their rules explicit, determine the hidden strategies, and make the disguised objectives clear and specific.

6. 1) The Passion Cluster—fascination, exclusiveness, and sexual desire; 2) the Caring Cluster—giving the utmost and being an advocate for one's partner.

CHAPTER 5

SINGLEHOOD, DATING, AND MATE SELECTION

CHAPTER OUTLINE

Being Single
    Increasing Singlehood
    Singlehood As an Alternative to Marriage
    The Pros and Cons of Singlehood
    Characteristics of Successful Singles
    Singles and Sexual Intimacy
    Singles and Loneliness
    Making Singlehood Work

Finding a Mate: Courtship Patterns
    Parent-Arranged Marriages
    The American Dating System

Criteria for Choosing a Mate
    Physical Attractiveness
    Age and Success Criteria
    Endogamy and Exogamy
    Intercultural Marriages in the United States

Theories of Mate Selection
    Homogamy Versus Complementarity
    Filter Theory
    Stimulus-Value-Role Theory
    Reiss's Wheel Theory of Love

Conflict and Violence in Dating
    Conflict Issues
    Courtship Violence
    Courtship Violence and Later Spouse Abuse

LEARNING OBJECTIVES

After reading Chapter 5, you should be able to:
- Describe the pros and cons of singlehood
- Outline the characteristics of successful singles
- Discuss issues involving singles and sexual intimacy
- Understand the difficulty of finding "Mr. Right" or "Ms. Right" and some of the services our society has developed to help with this process
- Compare "love matches" and arranged marriages and discuss how both are related to the double standard
- Summarize theories about mate selection, including the importance of physical attraction, age differences, and ethnic differences
- Explain the basic function of dating
- Discuss conflict and violence in dating relationships
- Discuss similarities and differences in dating patterns and practices between older individuals and younger individuals

PRACTICE TESTS

Key Terms

1. In a(n) _____, the marriage partner is selected by the parents of the bride and groom rather than by the partners.

2. The greater difficulty of older women than of older men in finding a mate involves a(n) _____, given that women tend to marry men who are better educated or more successful whereas men tend to marry women with less status who are younger than they are.

3. A couple is likely to engage in _____ after having developed rapport between them.

4. Mate selection based on individuals being attracted to people with personalities opposite to their own is part of the _____ theory.

5. The final process in the development of love in Reiss's theory of love is _____, which has to do with intimacy coming from having one's personal needs fulfilled.

6. The cultural practice or tradition of individuals choosing their mates from within their own groups, such as the same ethnic, religious, social class, or age group, is _____.

7. _____, or individual-choice courtship, is becoming more common in societies changing from agrarian to industrial.

8. The influence of _____, or nearness in time and space, on the pool of available partners is part of the filter theory of mate selection.

9. _____, the third process in the development of love, according to Reiss, occurs when each person in the relationship wants and needs the other person.

10. The number of men in a society relative to the number of women is the _____ in the society.

11. Two people who develop a sense of closeness and understanding may have _____.

12. _____ is the cultural tradition of individuals choosing their mates from outside their own group, such as from other religious or ethnic groups.

13. _____, becoming more common in dating, refers to the level of physical intimacy prior to marriage.

14. Even though it has lessened, there still remains a _____ expressed in different standards of sexual and social behavior for men than for women.

15. The tendency to marry someone of a similar or the same ethnic group, educational level, socioeconomic status, religion, and/or values is referred to as _____.

Multiple Choice

1. _____ is one reason divorce takes place in societies in which parent-arranged marriages are the norm.
   a. Infidelity
   b. Infertility
   c. A loveless marriage
   d. Incompatibility

2. The major influence away from parent-arranged marriages is:
   a. the mass media
   b. women's liberation
   c. the greater value placed on love
   d. industrialization

3. One of the largest problems for singles is:
   a. employment discrimination
   b. loneliness
   c. missing have children
   d. developing a network of people with whom to share social activities

4. Which society is mentioned in the text as relying less on matchmakers than in the past and as moving more toward love-based marriages as women have been gaining financial independence in the labor force?
   a. China
   b. Japan
   c. Sweden
   d. India

5. Which society is mentioned in the text as having experienced a steep decline in the marriage rate?
   a. China
   b. Japan
   c. Sweden
   d. India

6. Research conducted by Bulcroft and O'Conner-Roden indicates that older individuals (over the age of 60) are like younger people in dating except for:
   a. experiencing the "sweaty palm" syndrome
   b. anticipation of the date
   c. the need for intimacy
   d. the definition of dating

7. The age difference between males and females in first marriages is currently:
   a. about one year
   b. less than two years
   c. three years
   d. four years

8. Currently, there are about _____ single men for every 100 single women in the United States.
   a. 94
   b. 106
   c. 115
   d. 127

9. Principles of _____ make it likely that people from the same ethnic group will marry one another rather than someone of a different ethnic group.
   a. endogamy
   b. exogamy
   c. homogamy
   d. heterogamy

10. Which theory of mate selection relies on the concept of propinquity as a major influence?
    a. homogamy
    b. complementarity
    c. filter
    d. SVR

11. Which theory of mate selection has been criticized extensively based on there being little evidence to support it?
    a. homogamy
    b. complementarity
    c. filter
    d. exchange

12. Adolescent victims of violence often:
    a. define abuse as love
    b. assume problems will go away
    c. believe that violence is a consequence of intense love
    d. all of the above

13. The _____ theory of mate selection focuses on the testing of suitability for marriage following an initial attraction.
    a. complementarity
    b. SVR
    c. wheel
    d. exchange

14. According to a study by Springer, Fournier, and Olson, the number one (overall) source of relational conflict is:
    a. communication
    b. power
    c. personality
    d. time

15. What percentage of spouses who report physical abuse were abused during the courtship?
    a. 14 percent
    b. 27 percent
    c. 49 percent
    d. 72 percent

True/False

1. The percentage of single, adult individuals living with their parents has declined between 1960 and today.

2. Parent-arranged marriages are currently practiced, even preferred, in many of the nonindustrialized countries in the world.

3. Parent-arranged marriages tend to strengthen and reinforce community life.

4. According to Shostak, research indicates that individuals are more likely to have positive attitudes about singlehood if they have experienced divorce in their family.

5. Dating, as an institution, has existed in one form or another for centuries.

6. Women who remain single are more likely to be intelligent, successful individuals than women who marry.

7. Research conducted with men and women indicates that both cite a blend of physical and personal qualities when describing the qualities of an ideal sexual partner.

8. The importance of physical attractiveness to sexual satisfaction for men appears to persist even after years of marriage.

9. The percentage of black-white marriages has increased substantially following the Supreme Court's 1967 ruling declaring interracial marriages constitutional.

Short Answers

1. Name three advantages of parent-arranged marriages.

2. Identify Winch's six functions of dating.

3. What are three negative reasons for getting married as discussed in the text?

4. Name and briefly describe the three components of Murstein's SVR theory of mate selection.

5. Identify and describe the four processes involved in Reiss's Wheel Theory of Love.

6. Define *endogamy* and *exogamy* and explain the difference, including why this impacts mate selection.

Name _____   Chapter 5

PERSONAL INVOLVEMENT ASSESSMENT—
PROBLEMS AND ADVANTAGES OF BEING SINGLE

Back in the middle 1970s, sociologist Peter Stein interviewed single people, many of whom related the dark side of single life and others the bright side. Some examples of what he was told follow.[1]

Problems. A young woman employed as a computer programmer:

> My boss couldn't, or didn't want to, understand why I was not married. He imagines all sorts of orgies going on. Two of the younger guys (in the office) said they felt sorry for me, that I was missing out on a lot of fun. When I told them that I was happy and that I neither wanted to marry nor be a mother, they looked upset. . . . They couldn't understand my position and I think they didn't believe me. I was pretty upset by it.

Another young woman:

> When I'm friends with married people, I have to be very careful in how I act around husbands. Either one or both might think I'm coming on to the husband, when I'm really not.

A man who was an assistant professor at a university:

> It was hard being the only single person in the department. I would be invited to social gatherings and would get pretty nervous about who my date should be. The men would get into shop talk and the women, in some other part of the house, would talk about their families, the school system, and summer vacations. My date and I would usually feel uneasy, not quite fitting in and yet feeling a bit guilty about not fitting in.

A woman of 28:

> When I tell people I'm 28 and not married, they look at me like there's something wrong with me—they think I'm a lesbian. Some just feel sorry for me. What a drag.

A man of 35:

> [I am under] a non-specific pressure, a sort of wonderment that I can still be alone. I sometimes feel pressure from my own confusion of how come I don't conform to the patterns of people who are in the same situation as I am in terms of career and age.

Advantages. A young man:

> There aren't any conditions under which I would consider getting married. . . . I want freedom of choice, freedom to do what I want to do instead of being tied to just one person and doing the same . . . things over and over.

A young woman:

> There are so many things I want to do. Now that I've completed school and am making a good living, there is fun to be had. I've started a dance class, learned pottery, and joined a women's group.

A man who is again a bachelor after two marriages:

> I am having an experience I never had before, since I was always answerable to someone—my family or wife. I never had the experience of being completely self-motivated, having to consider someone else's reaction to what I do—approval, disapproval, does the job pay enough? It makes me feel potent . . . and very responsible for what I do. Productive, capable of dealing with life's exigencies, and capable even of seeking friendly help when I need it. Whether you are self-realized or not cannot be blamed on or credited to someone else.

Another man:

> Clown, promoter, radical, friend, playboy, priest . . . you name it, the possibilities are there. I'm in a situation to discover my potentialities and act on them. It's an exciting process—sometimes frightening, but I like having alternatives to choose from.

---

[1] P. J. Stein, "Singlehood: An Alternative to Marriage," *Family Coordinator* 24 (1975): 489–503. Copyright © 1975 by the National Council on Family Relations, 3989 Central Ave., NE, Suite 550, Minneapolis, MN 55421. Reprinted by permission.

Assessment. Think about the preceding examples. Have you had similar thoughts to any of those expressed? Are these examples relevant to problems and advantages experienced by singles *now?* Describe three examples of problems you believe are particularly pressing for today's singles.

1.

2.

3.

Name _____   Chapter 5

KNOWLEDGE IN ACTION—
VARIATIONS IN DATING AND COURTSHIP PRACTICES

As brought out in Chapter 5, dating is practiced mainly in Western countries. It is also a relatively new phenomenon; it evolved in the late nineteenth century, when the choice of a marriage partner became an individual decision rather than a family one. Observers of dating and courtship practices have noted continual change in these practices, including age that dating begins, opportunities for meeting the opposite sex, pattern of progression, degree of formality, reasons for dating, and gender roles in dating. Important differences exist, too, across social classes and racial and ethnic groups.[1] For example, "coming-out" parties for young women among the black elite are common in many urban areas. And dating among working-class youth tends to be unstructured, taking the form of "hanging around" in popular gathering spots, in contrast to the more structured dating more commonly practiced among middle-class and upper-class youth.

Project. Select one of the following two options for interviewing people about the variations in dating and courtship patterns.

Option 1: Generational Variation. Select any two of the changing areas in dating and courtship practices discussed in the text and develop open-ended interview questions pertaining to these topics. Your questions should concern interviewees' own dating and courtship experiences (if married, prior to marriage). Conduct interviews with several people representing different generational groups. Describe your sample (age, marital status, ethnicity, income and education level, etc.), report your findings, and discuss how they compare to the material presented in the text.

Option 2: Social Class and Racial/Ethnic Variation. Select any two of the changing areas in dating and courtship practices discussed in the text and develop open-ended interview questions pertaining to these topics. Your questions should concern interviewees' own dating and courtship experiences. Conduct interviews with several young people from different social classes and ethnic groups. Describe your sample (age, marital status, ethnicity, income and education level, etc.), report your findings, and discuss how they compare to the material presented in the text.

Sample.

---

[1] Maxine Baca Zinn and D. Stanley Eitzin, *Diversity in Families,* 4th ed. (New York: HarperCollins, 1996).

Findings.

Discussion.

ANSWER KEY

Key Terms

1. parent-arranged marriage
2. mating gradient
3. self-revelation
4. complementary needs
5. intimacy need fulfillment
6. endogamy
7. Dating
8. propinquity
9. Mutual dependency
10. sex ratio
11. rapport
12. Exogamy
13. Permissiveness
14. double standard
15. homogamy

Multiple Choice

1. b
2. d
3. d
4. b
5. c
6. d
7. b
8. d
9. a
10. c
11. b
12. d
13. b
14. c
15. c

True/False

1. F
2. T
3. T
4. T
5. F
6. T
7. F
8. T
9. T

Suggested Responses to Short Answer Questions

1. 1) They tend to be more stable because they get support from the whole family; 2) divorce is almost unheard of; 3) there are fewer if any of the problems associated with "dating."

2. 1) Provides adolescents with training for adulthood; 2) is the focus for social activities beyond courtship; 3) permits youths to establish their prestige and social position among their peers; 4) helps young individuals transfer their emotional orientation from their parents to their peer group and learn to function autonomously; 5) enables youths to learn sex roles and develop their sexual identity; 6) fulfills the instrumental role of mate selection for marriage.

3. Pressure from parents, desire to leave home, fear of independence, loneliness, not having a sense of alternatives.

4. Stimulus: attraction of individuals by a particular stimulus that acts as a form of magnetism, drawing the couple together and providing an energizing of the relationship. Value complementarity: assessment of compatibility of basic beliefs and values, which becomes more important than the initial stimulus. Role complementarity: establishment of a cooperative role relationship, e.g., regarding authority, division of labor, expectations for the relationship.

5. 1) Rapport—process of communication in which understanding and a sense of closeness develop; 2) self-revelation—the disclosing of personal information about oneself; 3) mutual dependency—a mutual wanting and needing of each other; 4) intimacy need fulfillment—satisfaction from having personal needs fulfilled.

6. Endogamy refers to mate selection within one's own group, whereas exogamy refers to mate selection outside of one's group. Parents may disapprove of a marriage between different groups, divorce is more prevalent, and children are more likely to have relationship problems.

CHAPTER 6

SEXUAL INTIMACY

CHAPTER OUTLINE

Sex and Society: An Overview
    Sexuality, Sex, and Gender
    Historical Perspectives on Sex and Society
    Sexuality Across Cultures

American Sexual Behavior Surveyed
    The University of Chicago Study
    The *Janus Report*
    The *American Couples* Study
    Gay-Male and Lesbian Sexual Behavior Surveyed

Sex Education
    Consequences of Inadequate Sex Education
    Sex-Education Programs
    Sex Education and Parents
    Is Sex Education Effective?

Premarital Sexual Behavior
    Sexual Behavior Among Adolescents
    Sexual Behavior Among College Students

Marital and Extramarital Sexual Behavior
    Sex Within Marriage
    Extramarital Sex

Toward Sexual Health
    Sexual Problems and Dysfunctions
    Sex Therapy

LEARNING OBJECTIVES

After reading Chapter 6, you should be able to:

- Discuss the difference between the terms *sexual identity* and *sexuality* and explain how a person is defined as a sexual being
- Sort out the myths and realities about sexuality
- Explain why standards of sexual attractiveness and sexual techniques vary widely in different cultures
- Explain the discrepancy between the phrase "sex is everywhere" in our society and the statistics on sexual behavior
- Summarize how to put the spark back into a relationship whose sexual satisfaction has declined
- Discuss pros and cons of sexuality education programs in this country, why they are needed, and whether they work
- Discuss the risk of premarital sexual behavior and of extramarital sex
- Understand the relationship between sex and marriage and why sex is important to an intimate relationship
- Know the types of sexual problems and dysfunctions that occur and how a sex therapist or sex educator can help resolve them

PRACTICE TESTS

Key Terms

1. Sexual activity and behavior are what is currently referred to as _____.
2. A sexual dysfunction involving a man's inability to achieve or maintain an erection is called a(n) _____.
3. Women who are unable to reach an orgasm experience _____.
4. A sexual dysfunction characterized by internal pain or pain felt in the penis and/or testicles for the man or pain for the woman around her sexual organs during intercourse is _____.
5. Sexual behavior or the lack of it can become a(n) _____ when it leads to anxiety, frustration, and other areas of unhappiness in personal relationships.
6. An individual who is attracted sexually to both females and males has a(n) _____ orientation.
7. A female sexual dysfunction in which intercourse is prevented by involuntary spasms in the outer third of the vagina is _____.
8. _____ is a sexual dysfunction characterized by a long and strenuous effort being required to achieve orgasm.
9. A(n) _____ is a prohibition of intercourse between parents and children and between siblings and is found in most societies.
10. A person's identifying himself or herself as a heterosexual, homosexual, or bisexual has to do with his or her _____.
11. _____ can provide individuals with relief from sexual problems and dysfunctions through instruction in the art of lovemaking.
12. A man's inability to ejaculate in the woman's vagina is _____.
13. Psychological, interpersonal, environmental, and cultural factors can be related to a(n) _____.
14. _____ is a sexual dysfunction that is related to physiological factors.
15. Having a sexual orientation to people of the other gender is being _____.
16. The _____ offers sex therapy using four types of treatment ranging from a granting of permission to an individual to engage in a type of sexual behavior to intensive therapy.
17. A(n) _____ works with large groups of people offering instruction on general information and principals regarding sex.
18. A man's reaching orgasm too quickly for the female to achieve orgasm can be characteristic of _____.
19. The values, beliefs, and behaviors associated with our definition of ourselves as sexual beings are part of our _____.
20. A(n) _____ works with individuals, couples, or small groups of individuals and couples to help with alleviating sexual problems and/or dysfunctions.
21. A sexual dysfunction for women in which orgasm is achieved too quickly is _____.
22. A(n) _____ orientation is one involving sexual orientation to someone of the same gender.
23. Currently, _____ is the state of being male or female.
24. A phenomenon among two-job couples labeled by therapists as inhibited or hypoactive sexual desire is the _____.

Multiple Choice

1. One aspect of _____ is the type of sexual acts an individual enjoys.
   a. sex
   b. sexual activity
   c. sexuality
   d. sexual identity

2. In a 1989 Gallup poll of over 500 college students that was commissioned by the Christian Broadcasting Network, nearly _____ of the students said that their faith, even though important in their lives, had relatively little impact on their sexuality.
   a. 20 percent
   b. 40 percent
   c. 60 percent
   d. 80 percent

3. Over _____ of the college students surveyed in a 1989 Gallup poll indicated that to them nonmarital sex was not wrong.
   a. one-fourth
   b. one-half
   c. two-thirds
   d. three-fourths

4. Which of the following is NOT true regarding sexuality?
   a. Kissing is common in most societies.
   b. Most societies condemn forced sexual relations.
   c. In some societies, masturbation by adults is tolerated, but masturbation by children and adolescents is not.
   d. The frequency of sexual intercourse varies by society.

5. Using the People's Republic of China as an example of a very traditional society in which cultural beliefs and attitudes have changed, over _____ of the people surveyed now approve of extramarital affairs.
   a. 35 percent
   b. 50 percent
   c. 60 percent
   d. 85 percent

6. The _____ study found that Americans' sexual behavior is more traditional than the images coming from the popular media and fiction.
   a. Janus
   b. University of Chicago
   c. Gordon
   d. Blumstein and Schwartz

7. The _____ study has been the most comprehensive survey since the Kinsey studies.
   a. Janus
   b. University of Chicago
   c. Gordon
   d. Blumstein and Schwartz

8. According to the _____ study, cohabiting couples and gay male couples together less than two years are the most sexually active couples.
   a. Janus
   b. University of Chicago
   c. Gordon
   d. Blumstein and Schwartz

9. To what do the text's authors attribute the United States' being a country with major sexual problems, such as single mothers and AIDS?
   a. weak religious values
   b. decline in commitment to marriage and the family
   c. inadequate sex education
   d. ineffective use of contraception

10. According to the *Janus Report,* more than _____ percent of American adults favor sex education.
    a. 40
    b. 65
    c. 80
    d. 90

11. Which group does the *Janus Report* indicate as having the highest level of sexual activity?
    a. married couples
    b. divorced persons
    c. singles—never married
    d. no difference in rate

12. Hellmich's study of 815 men found that _____ is the most important thing in a man's life.
    a. sex
    b. career
    c. fortune
    d. marriage

13. According to Masters and his colleagues, an estimated _____ of all married couples have some type of sexual dysfunction at some time in their marriage.
    a. one-fourth
    b. one-third
    c. one-half
    d. two-thirds

14. Which sexual dysfunction is expressed by the male's being unable to ejaculate in the vagina despite having a firm erection and being highly sexually aroused?
    a. erectile dysfunction
    b. premature ejaculation
    c. ejaculatory incompetence
    d. retarded ejaculation

15. According to results found in the 1994 University of Chicago study, about what percentage have been faithful their entire marriage?
    a. 25% of men; 35% of women
    b. 40% of men; 50% of women
    c. 55% of men; 75% of women
    d. 75% of men; 85% of women

True/False

1. Less than 50 percent of married adults in a 1994 University of Chicago study reported being faithful in the past year.
2. Since the rise of science, sexual behavior and thinking about sex are no longer guided by religious teachings and cultural beliefs, even though people still refer to specific religious principles.
3. According to the 1993 Janus Report, sexual activity among heterosexuals has decreased overall as a result of the AIDS epidemic.
4. Sexual behavior is regulated in some way in ALL societies.
5. After age 60, women tend to be somewhat more sexually active than men.

6. Gender roles pertaining to sexual behavior—e.g., initiating sex—are universal across all cultures.
7. According to the *Janus Report,* most Americans learn about sex from their families.
8. Research indicates that although people may disagree about issues pertaining to sexuality, they agree that sex education should begin in the home.
9. Janus and Janus (1993) determined that conservative individuals are no less likely than liberal individuals to be sexually active.
10. Research indicates that although sex after marriage becomes less exciting the longer people are married, intimacy does not appear to diminish with time.

Short Answer

1. Identify and briefly describe Freud's five psychosexual stages of human development.

2. Name the four generalizations about homosexuality across cultures.

3. List four negative consequences associated with adolescent pregnancy.

4. What appear to be the two features of the most successful programs to reduce adolescent pregnancies in the United States and other Western nations?

5. Identify the four components of the PLISSIT Model of sex therapy.

Name _____   Chapter 6

PERSONAL INVOLVEMENT ASSESSMENT— WHAT'S YOUR LOVEMAKING IQ?

According to Arthur Foster, a marriage counselor and sex therapist, the following questions are the most frequently asked of him in his practice. Answer the questions and then check your answers against the correct ones. Last, check for your lovemaking IQ.

_____ 1. Who gets the most pleasure from lovemaking?
   a. men
   b. women
   c. Both sexes enjoy lovemaking equally.

_____ 2. Your lover says you're undersexed, whereas you think he's oversexed. Could you both be right?
   a. yes
   b. no

_____ 3. Overall, how satisfied are most married couples with their sexual relationship?
   a. dissatisfied
   b. highly satisfied
   c. moderately satisfied

_____ 4. What percentage of men fail to maintain an erection sufficient to achieve penetration during sex?
   a. 7
   b. 20
   c. 40
   d. 60
   e. 75
   f. 100

_____ 5. How much time does the average couple devote to foreplay before going on to intercourse?
   a. 5 minutes or less
   b. 6–10 minutes
   c. 11–15 minutes
   d. 16 minutes or more

_____ 6. An erection is a sure sign that a man is highly aroused.
   a. true
   b. false

_____ 7. Your lover likes you to touch his breasts. Does this mean he has homosexual tendencies?
   a. yes
   b. no

_____ 8. For the most part, male and female orgasms are identical.
   a. true
   b. false

_____ 9. On the average, how many minutes do most men maintain an erection after the penis enters the vagina?
   a. Less than one
   b. 1–5
   c. 5–10
   d. more than 10

Section reprinted from *Cosmopolitan,* July 1986, pp. 98, 100, 136. © Arthur Foster. Reprinted by permission of author.

___ 10. One night you're thrilled when your lover caresses you in a certain way. But the next time you have sex, the same touch is a total turnoff. What's wrong?
   a. You have any one of a number of sexual problems.
   b. Your lover is not sensitive to your needs.
   c. nothing

___ 11. How often do most couples make love?
   a. once a day or more
   b. 5–6 times a week
   c. 2–4 times a week
   d. once a week
   e. less than once a week

___ 12. Your lover wants to have anal sex. Are there any problems you should be aware of before you consent?
   a. yes
   b. no

___ 13. How many orgasms is it possible for a woman to have during a single lovemaking session?
   a. one
   b. 3–5
   c. as many as 10
   d. more than 10

___ 14. Although women have little sensation beyond the opening and outer third of the vagina, you're extremely turned on when your man thrusts deeply. Is your case unusual?
   a. yes
   b. no

___ 15. Who initiates lovemaking more often?
   a. men
   b. women

Answers:

1. (a) Men. In a national sampling of married couples, husbands and wives were asked separately to rate how much pleasure they derived from various lovemaking activities. Men scored higher on every single activity.

2. (b) No. Being undersexed or oversexed has more to do with conditioning or personality.

3. (c) According to a recent poll, a little less than half the American married population rated their sexual relationship as "moderately satisfying," one-third unsatisfactory, and the remainder highly satisfied.

4. (a) Seven percent, but the answer depends on interpretation. Nearly every man struggles with impotence at some time, but about 7 percent of men remain impotent for months, even years.

5. (c) Eleven to 15 minutes.

6. (b) False. Erections can occur at times when arousal is absent or mild. Conversely, a man may feel passionate and not obtain an erection.

7. (b) No. Male breasts have the same nerve endings for pleasure as female breasts.

8. (a) True. Except that males ejaculate during orgasm and females do not.

9. (b) According to a study conducted at the Phoenix Psychological Institute, approximately 40 percent of husbands maintain an erection for between 1 and 5 minutes, 18 percent for less than 1 minute, 27 percent between 5 and 10 minutes, and the remaining 15 percent for more than 10 minutes.

10. (c) Nothing is wrong. Body sensitivity continually changes.

11. (c) According to a recent poll, 49 percent of married couples reported they made love two to four times a week, 10 percent more often, 41 percent less often.

12. (a) Yes. The rectum was not designed for sexual purposes, so a lubricant will allow for more comfort. Also, to avoid infection, do not immediately proceed from anal to vaginal intercourse, and gentleness on the part of the male is vital to avoiding possible injury.

13. (d) Scientists have recorded as many as 50 female orgasms in a single lovemaking session.

14. (a) Yes. Some women, however, experience intense pleasure from deep pelvic pressure, especially those who have had children.

15. (a) Men. When polled, however, both men and women said they'd prefer initiating to be equally shared.

Scoring:

Give yourself one point for each question you answered correctly. The sum is your lovemaking IQ.

10–15 points: Excellent. Your partner is sure to revel in such a knowledgeable lover.

5–10 points: Average. A bit of homework could change your love life from so-so to super!

Less than 5 points: Shaky. By clinging to sexual myths, you're probably not enjoying lovemaking as fully as possible.

Name _____   Chapter 6

KNOWLEDGE IN ACTION—
SCREENING FOR AIDS

Human immunodeficiency virus (HIV) has become of special concern because we do not yet have a way to fight it and because once it manifests itself as full-blown AIDS it is invariably fatal. Many sex education programs now include discussion of ways to protect oneself from contracting AIDS, including the advice to choose your sex partner carefully. According to University of Connecticut psychologist Jeffrey D. Fisher, undergraduates have taken this warning to heart and try to learn about their partners before becoming sexually involved. Fisher laments, however, that undergraduates focus on the wrong things in getting to know about their partners. They tend to follow an "implicit personality theory" concerning a person's hometown, academic record, and major to determine the probability that their prospective partner is HIV-positive. Instead, Fisher and others recommend that potential sexual partners should ask direct questions to ascertain whether their potential partner has AIDS or other STDs.

Two barriers to ascertaining necessary screening information are truthfulness of prospective partners and anxiety, embarrassment, and misunderstanding related to asking the right questions. A study of college students in southern California found that many people lie about their sexual histories and their testing for the AIDS virus. Nearly 50 percent of the men and 40 percent of the women reported that they were untruthful about the number of their past sexual partners. Twenty percent of the men also reported that they had lied to prospective partners about being tested for the AIDS virus. College students have also related discomfort in discussing sexual histories with prospective partners. Overcoming these barriers can be instrumental in abating the spread of AIDS, whose course was predicted by the U.S. Surgeon General in 1991 to be "more heterosexual spread, more women, children, young people."

Newsweek (1991) offers the following questions as a starting point for people exploring each other's sexual histories prior to becoming sexually involved:

- Have you been tested for HIV or other STDs?
- How many sex partners have you had?
- Have you ever been with a prostitute?
- (For a woman to ask a man): Have you ever had sex with another man?
- Have you or your sex partners ever injected drugs?
- Have you ever had a transfusion of blood or blood products (particularly before 1985, when blood wasn't screened for HIV)?

Project. Copy the questions above and show them to several students, both male and female. Ask each of them to react to these questions in terms of (1) which of these questions, if any, they have posed or would pose to prospective sexual partners, (2) the adequacy of this set of questions, (3) any other screening information they have sought or would seek from prospective partners, (4) whether they felt that partners or prospective partners have been or would be truthful in their responses, and (5) (for those who have asked questions) how they felt about asking those questions. Summarize your findings and discuss them in comparison to the information reported in the *Newsweek* article.

Source for this section is "Safer Sex," *Newsweek,* 9 December 1991, 52–56.

Results.

Discussion.

ANSWER KEY

Key Terms

1. sex
2. erectile dysfunction
3. anorgasmia
4. painful intercourse
5. sexual dysfunction
6. bisexual
7. vaginismus
8. Retarded ejaculation
9. incest taboo
10. sexual identity
11. Sex therapy
12. ejaculatory incompetence
13. psychological sexual dysfunction
14. Organic sexual dysfunction
15. heterosexual
16. PLISSIT Model
17. sex educator
18. premature ejaculation
19. sexuality
20. sex therapist
21. rapid orgasm
22. homosexual
23. gender
24. DINS dilemma

Multiple Choice

1. c
2. d
3. c
4. c
5. d
6. b
7. b
8. d
9. c
10. c
11. a
12. d
13. c
14. c
15. d

True/False

1. F
2. F
3. F
4. T
5. F
6. F
7. F
8. T
9. F
10. T

Suggested Responses to Short Answer Questions

1. Oral stage: birth–18 months—pleasure-seeking activities involving the mouth; anal stage: 1 1/2–3 years—pleasure seeking centered around anus and function of elimination; phallic stage: 3–6 years—pleasure seeking involves genitals, and child competes with parent of opposite sex (Oedipal complex); latency stage: 6–puberty—repression of sexual thoughts and focus on development of social and intellectual skills; genital stage: puberty–adulthood—renewed interest in sexuality.

2. 1) Homosexuality is universal; 2) homosexuality is more common among males than among females; 3) homosexuality is never the predominant form of sexual behavior for adults; 4) only about 5 percent or less of the population of any culture tends to practice homosexuality.

3. The father is absent and the mother rears the child alone, often placing a burden on the grandparents; the mother is less likely to continue in school; the mother has serious financial problems, inadequate housing, lack of transportation, and suffers loneliness, poor nutrition, physical health problems, and other stressors that foster child abuse and neglect.

4. Encourage abstinence but also offer alternatives, e.g., contraceptives, for those who choose to become sexually active.

5. 1) Permission-giving, 2) Limited Information, 3) Specific Suggestions, 4) Intensive Therapy

CHAPTER 7

GENDER ROLES AND POWER IN THE FAMILY

CHAPTER OUTLINE

Gender Roles
- International Survey and Male/Female Traits
- Traditional Versus Contemporary Views of Gender Roles
- International Perspectives on Gender Roles

Multicultural Perspectives on Gender Roles
- The Anthropological Perspective
- Mexican American Culture
- African American Culture
- Native American Culture
- Japanese Culture

Theories About Gender-Role Development
- Social Learning Theory
- Cognitive Development Theory
- Family Systems Theory
- Feminist Theory

Power in Families
- A Family Power Model
- Types of Power Patterns
- Power, Marital Satisfaction, and Mental Health
- Communication and Power Dynamics
- Suggestions from Family Therapists

LEARNING OBJECTIVES

After reading Chapter 7, you should be able to:
- Discuss the research on gender roles within the family, which points out that gender-based segregation of labor in families is still relatively common
- Review the research on power in families, showing how men still have more power than women and how this disparity is related to the devaluation of "women's work"
- Demonstrate how this disparity in power has negative consequences for intimate relationships, describing how when one spouse has more power than the other, the fragile bond of friendship between the two can be stretched to the breaking point
- Offer ideas on how a workable balance of power can be created between partners
- Know how to keep a relatively even balance of power in a relationship and why this is important

PRACTICE TESTS

Key Terms

1. An individual's freedom to assume both masculine and feminine roles is _____.
2. When one is able to change the behavior of others, one has _____.
3. Conversation in which each partner adopts a different tactic—one submissive, one dominant—reflects _____.
4. The _____ pertains to the relative power one spouse has over the other based on the relative amount of resources he or she has.
5. _____ occurs when individuals' thinking and organizing of their social lives revolves around stereotypes.
6. A(n) _____ exists when authority is shared in a relationship.
7. A(n) _____ refers to an overgeneralization about individuals based on their gender.
8. _____ are becoming more the norm now than in the past in male-female family roles.
9. Escalating of conflict occurs when _____ is used in discussions.
10. A win-win situation for couples can occur when they utilize a _____ type of discussion.
11. Focusing on thought processes as being critical, _____ maintains that children create gender identity and stereotypes while learning to understand the world around them.
12. When each spouse has about equal authority in a relationship, but in different areas, the couple has a(n) _____.
13. _____ focuses on the internalization of and reinforcement by others of gender-related behavior.
14. Marriages in which men have the primary authority have a _____.
15. The _____ role is assigned to men in Parsons's theory of the family.
16. _____ occurs when an individual is able to effect change on the part of other family members.
17. _____ is a set of traits traditionally associated with being male in a given society.
18. The sense of being male or female in one's society is _____.
19. According to Parsons's theory of the family, the _____ role is functionally performed by women.
20. A(n) _____ involves similar types of messages given by both spouses, even though their tactics may differ.
21. A(n) _____ is found in marriages in which women have the primary authority.
22. Both partners try to give control of the situation to the other when engaged in _____.
23. Traits traditionally associated with being female in a given society comprise _____.
24. Expectations for people's behaviors and responsibilities based on their being male or female comprise one's _____.

Multiple Choice

1. Referring to an attractive 16-year-old girl one has just met as a "beauty queen, a knock-out" could be an example of:
   a. gender
   b. gender role
   c. gender-role stereotyping
   d. gender identity

2. Which of the following is NOT true of the concept of androgyny?
   a. It is a combination of masculine and feminine characteristics in the same individual.
   b. Anatomy is destiny.
   c. It can help people survive in life.
   d. It avoids rigid assignment of roles to males and females.

3. According to Olson and colleagues (1989), which couples are the least egalitarian?
   a. young couples without children
   b. childbearing couples
   c. couples with adolescents
   d. retired couples

4. A *USA Today* poll (Ehrlich, 1984) found that _____ were the most clearly gender-segregated tasks for families.
   a. childrearing tasks
   b. financial-management tasks
   c. household-chores tasks
   d. vacation-planning tasks

5. According to Blumstein and Schwartz (1983) in their study of nearly 3,000 couples, _____ husbands were most opposed to helping out with housework.
   a. working-class
   b. middle-class
   c. upper-middle-class
   d. no difference by class

6. Which of the following was a finding of Margaret Mead in her classic study of sex and temperament in three New Guinea tribes?
   a. Gender roles differed in New Guinea in contrast to those found in American culture.
   b. Gender roles in New Guinea were found to parallel those found in American culture.
   c. Gender roles in New Guinea demonstrated cross-cultural differences.
   d. Gender roles in New Guinea were biological in origin.

7. A reason why some African American women do not accept a feminist agenda is:
   a. They are hesitant to conflict with African American males who share their racial oppression.
   b. They have been less likely to experience the housewife role.
   c. They no longer see a need for a strong women's movement.
   d. both a and b

8. Spouses express power in their interactions in several different ways. The interaction in which one partner is dominant and one is submissive is called:
   a. competitive symmetry
   b. submissive symmetry
   c. complementary interaction
   d. neutralized symmetry

9. In which culture do traditions make it difficult for the women to attain leadership roles?
    a. African American
    b. Mexican American
    c. Native American
    d. Asian American

10. Which of the following theories of gender-role development argues that gender-role stereotypes are used by young children to understand their gender identity?
    a. social learning
    b. cognitive development
    c. family systems
    d. feminist

11. Which of the following theories about gender-role development focuses on change?
    a. social learning
    b. cognitive development
    c. family systems
    d. feminist

12. Which of the following was NOT mentioned in the text as viewed consistently by social scientists as one of the most important resources affecting the balance of power in a relationship?
    a. income
    b. educational level
    c. attractiveness
    d. occupational status

13. Which type of power is exemplified by an individual's being influenced by someone viewed as particularly physically attractive?
    a. referent
    b. expert
    c. reward
    d. coercive

14. According to Craddock (1984), the happiest premarital couples are those in which:
    a. both partners are egalitarian
    b. both partners are traditional
    c. the male is egalitarian and the female is traditional
    d. the female is egalitarian and the male is traditional

True/False

1. For the most part, gender-based segregation of labor in the home has lessened dramatically over the past three decades.
2. A more egalitarian distribution of housework and child care is likely to result in a reversal of power from a male-centered power structure to a female-centered power structure.
3. Talcott Parsons's theory of gender roles in the family is still widely accepted among social scientists.
4. Evidence of the decline of the "double standard" is provided in the egalitarian roles of younger couples in contrast to those of older couples.
5. Early reinforcement of gender-related behavior by others is a major focus of the social learning theory of gender-role development.
6. According to Blumstein and Schwartz (1983) in their study of over 3,000 couples, equality in relationships appears to be easier in gay and lesbian couples than in heterosexual couples.

7. Machismo, or male exhibition of aggressiveness, is the predominant pattern for Mexican American males living in the United States.

8. Research clearly shows that power in families is a personal characteristic of a family member, not a feature of a family system.

9. Family systems that are rigid and enmeshed on the Circumplex Model tend to be less open to change and more dependent on one another.

10. Spouses are more likely to experience high levels of depression in marriages with an unequal division of decision-making power than in more equitable relationships.

Short Answer

1. According to the authors, why is it more appropriate to talk about "the other gender" than "the opposite sex"?

2. How has Parsons's theory of instrumental and expressive family roles been criticized?

3. What are the consequences of "The Second Shift" as reported by Hochschild (1989)?

4. What have cross-cultural studies indicated about family roles of women and men?

5. Describe Bem's utopian society beyond gender polarization.

Name _____   Chapter 7

PERSONAL INVOLVEMENT ASSESSMENT—
WHY I (STILL) WANT A WIFE

Regardless of whether you are a woman or a man, do you ever think how nice it would be to have your own personal assistant—someone who would be available to you at all times to take care of all your needs? Read over the following article, written by a **woman** who wishes she had such a person, in fact, a **wife**!

I belong to that classification of people known as wives. I am A Wife. And, not altogether incidentally, I am a mother. Not too long ago a male friend of mine appeared on the scene fresh from a recent divorce. He had one child, who is, of course, with his ex-wife. He is obviously looking for another wife. As I thought about him while I was ironing one evening, it suddenly occurred to me that I, too, would like to have a wife. Why do I want a wife?

I would like to go back to school so that I can become economically independent, support myself, and, if need be, support those dependent upon me. I want a wife who will work and send me to school. And while I am going to school I want a wife to take care of my children. I want a wife to keep track of the children's doctor and dentist appointments. And to keep track of mine, too. I want a wife to make sure my children eat properly and are kept clean. I want a wife who will wash the children's clothes and keep them mended. I want a wife who is a good nurturant attendant to my children, who arranges for their schooling, makes sure that they have an adequate social life with their peers, takes them to the park, the zoo, etc. I want a wife who takes care of the children when they are sick, a wife who arranges to be around when the children need special care, because, of course, I cannot miss classes at school. My wife must arrange to lose time at work and not lose the job. It may mean a small cut in my wife's income from time to time, but I guess I can tolerate that. Needless to say, my wife will arrange and pay for the care of the children while my wife is working.

I want a wife who will take care of *my* physical needs. I want a wife who will keep my house clean. A wife who will pick up after me. I want a wife who will keep my clothes clean, ironed, mended, replaced when need be, and who will see to it that my personal things are kept in their proper place so that I can find what I need the minute I need it. I want a wife who cooks the meals, a wife who is a *good* cook. I want a wife who will plan the menus, do the necessary grocery shopping, prepare the meals, serve them pleasantly, and then do the cleaning up while I do my studying. I want a wife who will care for me when I am sick and sympathize with my pain and loss of time from school. I want a wife to go along when our family takes a vacation so that someone can continue to care for me and my children when I need a rest and change of scene.

I want a wife who will not bother me with rambling complaints about a wife's duties. But I want a wife who will listen to me when I feel the need to explain a rather difficult point I have come across in my course of studies. And I want a wife who will type my papers for me when I have written them.

I want a wife who will take care of the details of my social life. When my wife and I are invited out by my friends, I want a wife who will take care of the babysitting arrangements. When I meet people at school that I like and want to entertain, I want a wife who will have the house clean, will prepare a special meal, serve it to me and my friends, and not interrupt when I talk about the things that interest me and my friends. I want a wife who will have arranged that the children are fed and ready for bed before my guests arrive so the children do not bother us.

And I want a wife who knows that sometimes I need a night out by myself.

I want a wife who is sensitive to my sexual needs, a wife who makes love passionately and eagerly when I feel like it, a wife who makes sure that I am satisfied. And, of course, I want a wife who will not demand sexual attention when I am not in the mood for it. I want a wife who assumes the complete responsibility for birth control, because I do not want more children. I want a wife who will remain sexually faithful to me so that I do not have to clutter up my intellectual life with jealousies. And I want a wife who understands that *my* sexual needs may entail more than strict adherence to monogamy. I must, after all, be able to relate to people as fully as possible.

If, by chance, I find another person more suitable as a wife than the wife I already have, I want the liberty to replace my present wife with another one. Naturally, I will expect a fresh, new life; my wife will take the children and be solely responsible for them so that I am left free.

When I am through with school and have a job, I want my wife to quit working and remain at home so that my wife can more fully and completely take care of a wife's duties.

My God, who *wouldn't* want a wife?

From *Ms.*, July/August 1990, p. 17. Copyright © 1971 by Judy Brady. Reprinted by permission of the author.

Assessment. Now, write about how you reacted to the article. Specifically, if you are a woman or a man, how would you like to have a **spouse** such as Judy Brady described? Should such a spouse only be a wife? What about this type of spouse being a husband? What do you think about anyone—male or female— having this role in a marriage?

Name _____   Chapter 7

KNOWLEDGE IN ACTION—
GENDER SOCIALIZATION

As discussed in the chapter, children develop their gender identity and take on gender roles as a result of at least some environmental influences. Concepts of masculinity and femininity vary, depending upon the culture and the society in which one lives as well as upon demographic factors and the social groups to which one belongs.

Project. For this exercise, select *one* area of influence on children's development of gender identity and learning of gender roles. Some suggestions are television cartoons, commercials, programs, MTV; magazine advertisements; children's picture books; comic books; toys and toy packaging, toy sections of catalogs; computer software; video games.

Conduct a *content analysis* of a sample of whatever area of influence you have selected. For example, look over 10 children's picture books selected at random at a library or belonging to a child you know; watch two hours of Saturday morning television, switching channels each half-hour; compare ads in a girl-oriented magazine with those in a boy-oriented magazine and with those in a gender-neutral magazine.

Develop a list of items to check—for example, numbers of males or females presented in major vs. minor roles and in specific male/female stereotypical roles. Tally the relative numbers found, and note some of the more explicit examples.

Analyze and summarize your findings.

Tally.

Analysis.

Summary/Implications of Findings.

(Attach another sheet of paper if necessary.)

ANSWER KEY

Key Terms

1. androgyny
2. power
3. complementary interaction
4. resource theory of family power
5. Gender polarization
6. syncratic power pattern
7. gender-role stereotype
8. Egalitarian roles
9. competitive symmetry
10. neutralized symmetry
11. cognitive development theory
12. autonomic power pattern
13. Social learning theory
14. husband-dominant power pattern
15. instrumental
16. Family power
17. Masculinity
18. gender identity
19. expressive
20. symmetrical interaction
21. wife-dominant power pattern
22. submissive symmetry
23. femininity
24. gender role

Multiple Choice

1. c
2. b
3. d
4. c
5. a
6. c
7. d
8. c
9. c
10. b
11. c
12. c
13. a
14. a

True/False

1. F
2. F
3. F
4. T
5. T
6. T
7. F
8. F
9. T
10. T

Suggested Responses to Short Answer Questions

1. The term "the opposite sex" accentuates differences and reinforces a hierarchical tradition based on sex.

2. Parsons's belief that society requires men to be instrumental and women to be expressive does not account for change, conflict, and dysfunction. It also fosters stereotypes and denigration of women.

3. Chronic exhaustion, low sex drive, and more frequent illness on the part of the wife; reduced health, happiness, and vitality of the marriage on the part of both partners.

4. Women have been the primary caretakers of children; men have been more likely to assume leadership roles in the economic and political arenas.

5. A society in which there would be no gender polarization except for reproduction purposes and no distinction between psychological and sexual natures of males and females. There would be no bondage of gender nor inequality.

CHAPTER 8

COMMUNICATION AND INTIMACY

CHAPTER OUTLINE

Perspectives on Communication
    Gender Differences in Communication Style
    Cultural Differences in Communication Style

Using Communication to Develop Intimacy
    Communication As a Cooperative Endeavor
    Content and Relationship Messages
    Nonverbal Communication
    Mixed Messages and Double Binds
    Metacommunication: Clarifying Your Communication

Using Communication to Maintain Intimacy
    Speaking: The Art of Self-Disclosure
    Listening: A Difficult Skill
    Passive, Aggressive, and Assertive Communication

Types of Talk
    Small Talk and Shop Talk
    Control Talk
    Search Talk
    Straight Talk

LEARNING OBJECTIVES

After reading Chapter 8, you should be able to:
- Describe the importance of communication in developing and maintaining intimacy
- Recognize how styles of communication used by males and females and by various cultural groups differ
- Discuss the basic principles of communication and the importance of nonverbal communication
- Identify specific speaking and listening skills and explain how to use them effectively
- Explain the value of assertiveness and the usefulness of various styles of communication
- Discuss the term *self-disclose* and how it can enhance mental health

PRACTICE TESTS

Key Terms

1. _____ reinforces feelings of low self-esteem and limits expressiveness.
2. The more clearly defined a relationship is, the less chance there is of a(n) _____ message occurring.
3. The _____ of interpersonal communication espouses there being a responsibility on the part of both persons for what happens.
4. _____ reinforces positive feelings of self-esteem and encourages expressiveness in the other person.
5. The type of talk that involves straightforward communication and a commitment to positive future action is _____.
6. Conversation focusing on work-related matters is _____.
7. A discrepancy existing between the verbal and the nonverbal components in communication is referred to as a(n) _____.
8. _____ involves the LEAST amount of actual listening of all types of listening.
9. _____ is a type of talk that often reflects complaining and low self-esteem.
10. _____ attempts to channel the conversation rather than fully engaging in taking in what the other person is saying.
11. _____ is a type of talk whose purpose is to explore facts and possibilities in a rational way.
12. _____ is found in spoken communication as well as in written communication.
13. _____ occurs when an individual willingly communicates some information about himself or herself that other people would otherwise not know.
14. A very common type of talk intended to gain agreement or compliance is _____.
15. Communicating about communication, or _____, can help prevent a double bind from occurring.
16. The type of everyday communication engaged in by most people is _____.
17. _____ is characterized by blame of the other person and involves self-enhancing expressiveness.
18. A model of interpersonal communication that espouses there being a direct relationship between cause and effect is the _____.
19. The type of talk that typically leads to a negative response from others is _____.
20. _____ encourages communication on the part of the other person.

Multiple Choice

For questions 1–5, select either *a. males* or *b. females* to fit the type of communication skill listed.

1. Use good listening behaviors.
2. Use conversation in a competitive way.
3. Tend to talk more.
4. Use conversation in a more affiliative way.
5. Are more focused on responding.

6. A primary objective of straight talk is to:
   a. manipulate the person with whom you are having a conflict so that he or she can see your point.
   b. give each person a better understanding of complex, hard-to-define issues.
   c. develop a genuine connection so that a solution can evolve naturally.
   d. build a reservoir of pleasant times for both people to remember.

7. The _____ component of communication is usually straightforward and verbal in the way it is given.
   a. report
   b. relationship
   c. command
   d. causal

8. _____ refers to the means of getting out of a double bind situation.
   a. Metacommunication
   b. Assertiveness
   c. Circular causality
   d. Nonverbal communication

9. Which of the following is NOT one of the ten communication approaches that will destroy intimacy?
   a. Speak for yourself, not for others.
   b. Avoid talking about your relationship.
   c. Often talk about the weather and daily events.
   d. Assume any issue will disappear over time.

10. Which type of talk is reflected in the use of compliments, praise, persuasion, and directing?
    a. small talk
    b. shop talk
    c. control talk
    d. straight talk

11. Search talk is characterized by:
    a. trying to make a genuine connection with the other person.
    b. comfortable verbal exchanges in social situations.
    c. focusing on individuals rather than on their behavior or the issue at hand.
    d. objective, intellectual, and rational exploration of facts and possibilities.

12. A car salesperson is most likely to engage in which goal of listening?
    a. persuasive listening
    b. directive listening
    c. attentive listening

13. Which of the three goals of listening is likely to be the most efficient?
    a. persuasive listening
    b. directive listening
    c. attentive listening

14. _____ behavior is exemplified by the receiver's achieving the desired goal at the sender's expense.
    a. Passive
    b. Aggressive
    c. Assertive

15. Which of the following types of talk is most likely to occur as a result of anger and frustration?
    a. control
    b. fight
    c. spite
    d. search

True/False

1. Tannen concludes that women could learn some communication styles from men.
2. As found in the Gender Communication Quotient quiz, female managers communicate with more emotional openness and drama than male managers do.
3. Noncommunication is a form of communication.
4. The "blame game" is what occurs in a linear causality model rather than a circular causality model of interpersonal communication.
5. Many authorities indicate that about 30 percent of all face-to-face communication is nonverbal.
6. One's ability to be assertive is primarily related to one's personality style.
7. Double binds are more likely to occur if the relationship component is clear rather than unclear.
8. Self-disclosure requires the individual to be both aware of the information to be disclosed and predisposed to disclose the information.
9. Self-disclosure can be easier to engage in with strangers than with acquaintances and friends, depending on the circumstance.
10. Cultural expectations can lead to misinterpretation of nonverbals.

Short Answer

1. Contrast what Tannen found to be needs for intimacy and needs for independence in intimate relationships.

2. Provide two examples of cultural differences in communication styles.

3. How do children change communication in families?

4. What are three forms of nonverbal communication?

5. How can double binds be beneficial to a relationship?

Name _____   Chapter 8

PERSONAL INVOLVEMENT ASSESSMENT—
REBUILDING INTIMACY

According to Dr. Lori H. Gordon, many of the problems in couples' relationships stem from hurt feelings, miscommunication, and disillusionment. We get confused, hurt. As a result, we erect defenses against one another. Much of what we find disappointing in a partner has to do with what we perceive as his or her inability to listen without judging or giving advice that is unwanted. But do we too frequently have unrealistic expectations? Are we even completely aware of our own expectations? Do we genuinely communicate effectively our expectations of our partner?

To Dr. Gordon, we cannot achieve real and lasting relationships based on intimacy unless we are able to express our own thoughts and feelings as well as be able to listen to our partner's thoughts and feelings. She has found in her years of work with couples that too often what we do is engage in "mind reading." We expect in our new partner what we had experienced in our former relationships. Actions by our present partner that are in some way similar to those that were sources of problems in prior relationships can trigger emotional responses that exacerbate problems in the present. Dr. Gordon refers to this as "emotional allergy," resulting in withdrawal or counterattack that can be baffling to the current partner.

But, according to Gordon, there is something we can do about this. Her recommendations for changing hidden expectations formed from the past but affecting the present are:

- "If you expect a partner to understand what you need, then you have to tell him or her. That of course means you have to figure out for yourself what you really need.

- You cannot expect your partner to be sensitive and understand exactly how you feel about something unless you're able to communicate to him or her how you feel in the first place.

- If you don't understand or like what your partner is doing, ask about it and why he or she is doing it. And vice versa. Explore. Talk. Don't assume." (1993, p. 80)

To Dr. Gordon, confiding, though, does not mean just revealing yourself to another; rather, it is being confident that your partner is really hearing and understanding what it is you are thinking and feeling. This involves both telling what is really going on instead of telling what you think your partner wants to hear and listening *with empathy* to your partner—being attentive to your partner's emotions, facial expressions, displaying of tension. Don't anticipate and fill in the blanks or be passive in your listening—listen for what is in the mind and heart of your partner.

Dr. Gordon recommends an exercise that she adapted from a technique used by family therapist Virginia Satir. She calls it the Daily Temperature Reading, which helps partners learn to listen nondefensively and talk in such a way as to give information rather than to create an emotional reaction.

The Daily Temperature Reading:

"Sit close, perhaps even knee-to-knee, facing your partner, holding each other's hands. This simple touching creates an atmosphere of acceptance for both.

1. APPRECIATION. Take turns expressing appreciation for something your partner has done—and thanking each other.

2. NEW INFORMATION. In the absence of information, assumptions—often false ones—rush in. Tell your partner something ('I'm not looking forward to the monthly planning meeting this morning') to keep contact alive and let your partner in on your mood, your experiences—your life. And then listen to your partner.

3. PUZZLES. Take turns asking each other something you don't understand and your partner can explain: 'Why were you so down last night?' Or voice a question about yourself: 'I don't know why I got so angry while we were figuring out expenses.' You might not find answers, but you will be giving your partner some insight about yourself. Besides, your partner may have insights about your experiences.

Lori H. Gordon, "Intimacy: The Art of Working Out Your Relationships," *Psychology Today*, September/October 1993, pp. 40–43. Reprinted with permission from Psychology Today Magazine. Copyright © 1993 Sussex Publishers, Inc.

4. COMPLAINT WITH REQUEST FOR CHANGE. Without placing blame or being judgmental, cite a specific behavior that bothers you and state the behavior you are asking for instead. 'If you're going to be late for dinner tonight, please call me. That way the kids and I can make our own plans and won't be waiting for you.'

5. HOPES. Sharing hopes and dreams is integral to a relationship. Hopes can range from the mundane ('I hope you don't have to work this weekend') to the grandiose ('I'd really love to spend a month in Europe with you'). But the more the two of you bring dreams into immediate awareness, the more likely you'll find a way to realize them." (1993, p. 41)

Assessment. Answer the following questions based on Dr. Gordon's recommendations.

1. Mind Reading: Give two examples of mind reading in which you have engaged or that you have observed in others.

    a.

    b.

2. Emotional Allergy: Give two examples of emotional allergy—specific emotional reactions triggered by an action of someone that reminds you of something someone else did that bothered you in the past.

    a.

    b.

3. The Daily Temperature Reading: Try out this exercise with someone close to you—it doesn't have to be a spouse or partner; it could be a friend, parent, sibling, or someone else with whom you have a close relationship.

    a. Describe the experience.

    b. How did you feel doing it?

    c. How did the other person seem to feel doing it?

    d. Discuss your views on its value (or lack of value) as something couples could use on a regular basis for working out problems in their communication of thoughts and feelings.

Name _____   Chapter 8

KNOWLEDGE IN ACTION—
REPORT-TALK VERSUS RAPPORT-TALK

Chapter 8 identifies gender differences in communication styles. The text describes the source of the problem as different interests and differences in willingness to express sensitivity, based on gender-role socialization. Sociolinguist Deborah Tannen supports this claim with her extensive analysis of the different conversational styles of men and women in her book *You Just Don't Understand: Women and Men in Conversation.*

Tannen likens the distinction between male and female conversational styles to the difference between "report-talk" and "rapport-talk." Report-talk, favored by men, is a style in which the speaker exhibits knowledge and skill, often by holding center stage through storytelling, joking, or providing information. Even though report-talk seems most geared toward group conversations and public speaking, it is also used in private conversations. Rapport-talk, favored by women, emphasizes establishing connections and negotiating relationships by sharing details, personalizing conversations, and matching experiences. Rapport-talk personalizes the speaking situation when used in public situations.

Tannen maintains that these contrasting conversational styles help explain gender barriers in communication between the sexes. They represent not only different ways of talking but different content as well. Consider Tannen's example from a scene in the film *Divorce American Style*. When Debbie Reynolds complains that Dick Van Dyke doesn't tell her anything, he insists that he does. From each of their standpoints, they are right. He tells her everything that he regards as important information to tell a friend—report-talk style. But she expects his description of the goings-on of his day to include his feelings and thoughts, the same things she discusses with her female friends—rapport-talk style.

Project. Record three to five conversations. It doesn't matter whether or not you are a participant, but it would be both courteous and ethical to request permission from the participants prior to recording conversations. After you have completed your recordings, assign codes to the participants in each conversation and analyze statements and questions in terms of both the participant's gender and the conversational style—rapport or report. A sample tally sheet is provided to assist you with the analysis. Summarize your data and discuss potential gender differences in communication styles of males and females. Include a few quotes from your data to support your discussion.

SAMPLE TALLY SHEET

Speaker Code	Statement/Question	Gender Code	Style Code
1	I am having trouble deciding which candidate to vote for in the legislative primary.	2	2
2	It is not hard to decide if you just research the candidates' views on the major subjects, especially the subjects you care about.	1	1
3	You are not alone, Courtney; I am having trouble deciding too.	1	2

KEY:

Speaker	Code	Gender	Code	Style	Code
Courtney	1	Male	1	Report	1
Michael	2	Female	2	Rapport	2
Leroy	3				

Source for this section is Deborah Tannen, *You Just Don't Understand: Women and Men in Conversation* (New York: Ballantine, 1990).

Findings.

Discussion.

ANSWER KEY

Key Terms

1. Passive communication
2. double bind
3. circular causality model
4. Assertive communication
5. straight talk
6. shop talk
7. double message
8. Persuasive listening
9. Spite talk
10. Directive listening
11. Search talk
12. Nonverbal communication
13. Self-disclosure
14. control talk
15. metacommunication
16. small talk
17. Aggressive communication
18. linear causality model
19. fight talk
20. Attentive listening

Multiple Choice

1. b
2. a
3. a
4. b
5. a
6. c
7. a
8. a
9. a
10. c
11. d
12. b
13. c
14. a
15. b

True/False

1. T
2. F
3. T
4. T
5. F
6. F
7. F
8. F
9. T
10. T

Suggested Responses to Short Answer Questions

1. Women are more likely to have a need for intimacy, and men a need for independence. These differing needs reflect masculine culture and feminine culture.

2. Gestures are thought to be bold and undesirable in England, but they are common in Italy, France, and the Polynesian islands, for example. Physical displays of affection are interpreted differently by different cultures, and the ways in which men react to beautiful women vary from one culture to the next. Likewise, different gestures mean different things, as does directness of eye contact.

3. Complexities increase; positive communication becomes more important. Parents tend to rate communication quality as more problematic than do their adolescents.

4. Facial expressions, eye contact, gestures and other body movements, spatial behavior, body contact, nonverbal vocalizations, and posture.

5. They can call for a discussion clarifying the relationship. They can help the partners see the need for change in the relationship.

CHAPTER 9

CONFLICT AND CONFLICT RESOLUTION

CHAPTER OUTLINE

Conflict and Anger: An Overview
    The Hierarchy of Conflict
    Anger and Conflict Taboos
    Myths, Theories, and Facts About Anger

Intimacy and Conflict
    Intimacy Breeds Conflict
    Love and Anger in Balance
    The Dance of Anger
    Sources of Conflict in Couples

Approaches to Conflict Resolution
    Fighting Fair
    Constructive and Destructive Approaches
    Styles of Conflict Resolution
    Resolving Conflict: Six Basic Steps

LEARNING OBJECTIVES

After reading Chapter 9, you should be able to:

- Understand the importance of dealing positively with challenging situations and conflicts in life before they become crises
- Recognize that anger is a "normal" emotion, one that we all feel at times, but that it is not a particularly beneficial emotion, especially when we act out of anger. Reason is a much more useful tool for building healthy, intimate relationships.
- Demonstrate the process by which intimacy breeds conflict
- Outline the common issues over which couples often find themselves in conflict
- Explain constructive and destructive approaches to conflict resolution
- Discuss methods people use to manage their stress and anger

PRACTICE TESTS

Key Terms

1. Believing everyone else is responsible for his or her problems is what the _____ does.
2. A(n) _____ of conflict resolution involves putting one's own concerns above those of others.
3. _____ is a negotiating strategy used in bargaining in which agreements are based on each party's giving something.
4. _____ is reflected in acting as though one agrees with someone while privately disagreeing, but with hostility and aggressiveness eventually emerging.
5. A(n) _____ of conflict resolution involves each person giving a little.
6. Bringing _____, or resolution, to a disagreement helps restore bonding and respect in a relationship.
7. _____ is a negotiating strategy reflected in agreeing to do something the other person wants you to do in exchange for being able to do something you want to do.
8. Withholding one's true feelings from someone until they erupt in some form of attack is referred to as _____.
9. A(n) _____ seeks emotional space from his or her partner when feeling high levels of stress.
10. Some individuals use a(n) _____ of conflict resolution, meaning they try to withdraw or remain passive.
11. Being able to see the absurd in a situation is reflected in _____.
12. An individual who uses the _____ of conflict resolution tends to be nonassertive and cooperative.
13. The individual who tends to take charge and rescue others during times of stress is a(n) _____.
14. Showing concern for others while being assertive in reaching one's own goals involves a(n) _____ of conflict resolution.
15. An individual who seeks greater togetherness during a time of stress in a relationship is a(n) _____.
16. A(n) _____ becomes less competent under stress.
17. A(n) _____ exists when partners have difficulty finding a comfortable balance between separateness and togetherness, moving back and forth between extremes of enmeshment and disengagement.
18. A negotiating strategy used when a mutually agreeable solution cannot be found is _____.

Multiple Choice

1. According to the authors, a _____ operates on a continuum—from exchanges on daily events to crises.
   a. circumplex model
   b. conflict generation model
   c. hierarchy of conflict
   d. "dance of anger"

2. Which phase is marked by the highest level of tension when conflict occurs?
   a. problem solving
   b. expression of feeling
   c. discussion of ideas
   d. need for decision

3. Which phase in a conflict hierarchy is exemplified by a decision's being made that could turn out to be ineffective?
   a. problem solving
   b. expression of feeling
   c. discussion of ideas
   d. need for decision

4. According to Borcherdt, which human emotion has created the greatest destruction not only for individuals, couples, and families but also for social groups and nations?
   a. hate
   b. resentment
   c. anger
   d. guilt

5. According to Alberti and Emmons, which is a MYTH rather than a FACT concerning anger?
   a. Most anger is directed toward those close to us, not toward strangers.
   b. Anger is universal among human beings.
   c. Venting "releases" anger and therefore "deals with" it.
   d. Aggression leads to further aggression, not resolution.

6. The Circumplex Model describes people who value self-reliance and privacy as:
   a. pursuers
   b. distancers
   c. underfunctioners
   d. overfunctioners

7. _____ are likely to be inflexible but reliable, according to the Circumplex Model.
   a. Pursuers
   b. Distancers
   c. Underfunctioners
   d. Overfunctioners

8. Except for housework and child care, our society encourages women to be:
   a. pursuers and underfunctioners
   b. distancers and underfunctioners
   c. distancers and overfunctioners
   d. pursuers and overfunctioners

9. Our society encourages men to be:
   a. pursuers and underfunctioners
   b. distancers and underfunctioners
   c. distancers and overfunctioners
   d. pursuers and overfunctioners

10. In a longitudinal study of the changing nature of conflict in relationships, Bader and his colleagues found that progressively during the first five years of marriage, couples were most likely to be in conflict over:
    a. household tasks
    b. sex
    c. money
    d. time and attention

11. Crosby's rule for fair fighting that has to do with avoiding misperceptions is:
    a. owning your own feelings first
    b. avoiding accusations and attack
    c. checking out your own perceptions
    d. repeating the message you think you received

12. Which of the following is a destructive approach to resolving conflict?
    a. prevent stagnation
    b. accept mutual blame
    c. express feelings—both positive and negative
    d. focus on the person rather than the issue

13. The _____ style of conflict resolution is likely to be used by people who are highly assertive yet concerned for others.
    a. collaborative
    b. compromise
    c. accommodating
    d. competitive

14. Which strategy for negotiating within intimate relationships is characterized by keeping focused on the discussion?
    a. clarifying the issue
    b. finding out what each person wants
    c. identifying various alternatives
    d. solidifying the agreements

15. Omitting _____ as a strategy for negotiating within intimate relationships can often lead to unsatisfactory negotiations and repetitive fights.
    a. clarifying the issue
    b. finding out what each person wants
    c. identifying various alternatives
    d. reviewing and renegotiating

True/False

1. The more intimate the relationship, the more chances there are for interpersonal conflict.
2. Love is the opposite of hate.
3. The common divorce scenario is not fireworks as much as it is a gradual loss of closeness.
4. A couple in which one partner is an overfunctioner and the other is an underfunctioner is complementary.
5. Arond and Parker found that the fights of most newlyweds who fight last hours rather than minutes or days.
6. Crosby maintains that it is useful to refer to verbal conflicts as fights rather than to gloss over them.
7. In general, issuing ultimatums can be useful in "fair fighting," as long as both parties agree to this.
8. It is preferable to put off resolving very difficult issues, especially when one or both partners react emotionally to them.
9. Accommodation as a style of conflict resolution is marked by assertive and cooperative behavior.
10. According to Lerner, problems can arise when individuals let one way of managing anger dominate rather than find a balance among the several ways.

Short Answer

1. Name the three phases in the hierarchy of conflict and describe how each might look in a couple's involvement in a conflict situation over an episode of near infidelity.

2. Identify and contrast the two major reasons for suppressing negative emotions, according to Crosby.

3. Provide a counterpoint to each of the commonly held beliefs about anger, as identified by Borcherdt.

4. Describe the strategies couples can use to negotiate differences and the advantages and disadvantages of each.

5. Describe Lerner's "dance of anger."

Name _____   Chapter 9

PERSONAL INVOLVEMENT ASSESSMENT—
ABILITY TO TAKE CRITICISM

Part of the ability to communicate and to handle conflict includes being able to give and take criticism. There can be a fine line, however, between being *able* to handle criticism and *not* being able to do so. And, in fact, oftentimes the sharing of negative feelings and criticism with another person can create or increase tension, even within the most harmonious relationships.

Although criticism can be negative or constructive, how it is received can depend on *how* and *from whom* it is communicated.

Assessment. Answer the following questions pertaining to criticism and then compare your responses with the results from a survey conducted by Simmons Market Research (found on the next page).

1. From whom do you *least* appreciate receiving criticism? (Assign a number **in rank order**—a *1* for "least appreciate" up to an *11* for "most appreciate.")

    ____ spouse/partner

    ____ friends

    ____ parents

    ____ children

    ____ in-laws

    ____ grandparents/other relatives

    ____ employers

    ____ work subordinates

    ____ faculty

    ____ other students

    ____ other _____

2. Are you self-critical?

    ____ yes

    ____ no

3. It's harder to give criticism than to receive it.

    ____ agree

    ____ disagree

4. It's harder to receive criticism than to give it.

    ____ agree

    ____ disagree

5. It's as tough to give criticism as it is to receive it.

    ____ agree

    ____ disagree

From Karen S. Peterson, "We resent criticism from in-laws," *USA Today,* 24 October 1988. Copyright © 1988 USA Today. Used with permission.

Survey Results. According to results of a nationwide survey conducted with 500 professionals and managers, 24 percent listed criticism from *in-laws* as the *least* appreciated. The next most resented source of criticism was one's mate (22 percent), followed by work subordinates (21 percent). Other findings of the study conducted by Simmons Market Research include:

- Women (30 percent) have a harder time giving criticism than men (19 percent).

- Men (24 percent) resent criticism from their kids more than women (14 percent) do.

- Women (42 percent) are more likely to take corrective action following criticism from co-workers than are men (31 percent).

- Although 77 percent of all respondents were self-critical, women (85 percent) are more likely to be so than are men (71 percent).

- Twenty-four percent of both sexes believe it's just as tough to give criticism as it is to receive it.

Now, write about what, if anything, you found surprising about the survey results.

How did your responses compare to the results of the survey?

Name _____   Chapter 9

KNOWLEDGE IN ACTION—
RULES FOR FAIR FIGHTING

Marriage and relationships in general can be tough! It seems impossible to avoid having disagreements, even at times, fights. But, as Crosby has brought out and was discussed in Chapter 9, verbal disagreements can become serious, especially if they escalate into physical conflict. Crosby argues that it is important to maintain trust in our partner—that he or she will not abandon us or take advantage of us. Otherwise, people will not feel safe voicing disagreement, which can be productive. Crosby outlines 16 ground rules for fair fighting, all described in Box 9.3 in the chapter.

Project. First, reread the rule descriptions in Box 9.3. Then, for each of Crosby's 16 rules for fair fighting (found below), rate yourself on a continuum from 1 (low—you never adhere to this rule) to 5 (high—you always adhere to this rule). Third, indicate how important you believe it is or would be for you to follow this rule in voicing disagreements with a partner, from 1 (not important) to 5 (highly important). Fourth, give an example of what you typically tend to do in association with this rule.

		Adherence to Rule	**Importance to You**
1.	Negotiate from the Adult position.	1 2 3 4 5	1 2 3 4 5

Example:

2.	Avoid Ultimatums.	1 2 3 4 5	1 2 3 4 5

Example:

3.	If One Loses, Both Lose.	1 2 3 4 5	1 2 3 4 5

Example:

4.	Say What You Really Mean.	1 2 3 4 5	1 2 3 4 5

Example:

CONFLICT AND CONFLICT RESOLUTION   107

	Adherence to Rule	Importance to You
5. Avoid Accusations and Attack. Example:	1 2 3 4 5	1 2 3 4 5
6. Own Your Own Feelings First. Example:	1 2 3 4 5	1 2 3 4 5
7. Always Check Out Your Perceptions. Example:	1 2 3 4 5	1 2 3 4 5
8. State Your Wishes and Requests Clearly and Directly. Example:	1 2 3 4 5	1 2 3 4 5
9. Never Use Sex to Smooth Over a Disagreement. Example:	1 2 3 4 5	1 2 3 4 5
10. Repeat the Message You Think You Received. Example:	1 2 3 4 5	1 2 3 4 5

	Adherence to Rule	Importance to You
11. Refuse to Fight Dirty. Example:	1 2 3 4 5	1 2 3 4 5
12. Resist Giving the Silent Treatment. Example:	1 2 3 4 5	1 2 3 4 5
13. Focus on the Issue and Focus on the Present. Example:	1 2 3 4 5	1 2 3 4 5
14. Call "Time-Out" and "Foul." Example:	1 2 3 4 5	1 2 3 4 5
15. Use Humor and Comic Relief. Example:	1 2 3 4 5	1 2 3 4 5
16. Always Go for Closure. Example:	1 2 3 4 5	1 2 3 4 5

Last, compare your responses among the 16 rules for fair fighting. Discuss what you believe to be the areas most important to you in how you interact with your partner (or how you would interact with a partner) and what areas you would like to change.

ANSWER KEY

Key Terms

1. blamer
2. competitive style
3. Quid pro quo
4. Passive-aggressive behavior
5. compromise style
6. closure
7. Quid pro quid
8. gunnysacking
9. distancer
10. avoidance style
11. incongruity humor
12. accommodating style
13. overfunctioner
14. collaborative style
15. pursuer
16. underfunctioner
17. dance of anger
18. agreeing to disagree

Multiple Choice

1. c
2. a
3. a
4. c
5. c
6. b
7. d
8. a
9. c
10. a
11. c
12. d
13. a
14. a
15. b

True/False

1. T
2. F
3. T
4. F
5. F
6. T
7. F
8. F
9. F
10. T

Suggested Responses to Short Answer Questions

1. 1) Decision-making phase: discussions on how the one partner could avoid the other person, the couple's getting marital counseling, putting off a resolution; 2) problem-solving phase: if the affair has occurred, the couple might then begin or continue counseling, decide to separate, try terminating the affair; 3) crisis-resolution phase: terminate the affair, divorce, commit violence, etc.

2. 1) Sociological—cultural or social taboos against the emotion, e.g., anger, incestuous love; 2) psychological—human insecurity, in which individuals fear they will not be loved or accepted if people recognize their frailties.

3. 1) <u>Anger is caused by others</u>: Anger is self-created and usually occurs when someone does something we don't like.

    2) <u>The best way to deal with anger is to "let it all hang out"</u>: Venting can bring out the same feelings in others and does not resolve the underlying conflicts.

    3) <u>Anger is a beneficial emotion</u>: Anger can push others away in the long run and even make them want to get even.

    4) <u>You're a "wimp" if you don't get angry</u>: Strength is not measured by hostility and aggression.

4. 1) <u>quid pro quo</u>—this for that; dividing tasks equally.

    2) <u>quid pro quid</u>—this for this; doing something in exchange for being able to do something you want to do (or don't want to do). The consequences of not living up to the bargain are clearer than in quid pro quo.

    3) <u>agreeing to disagree</u>—putting off a solution until later; can work in noncritical issues but can be problematic in critical issues.

5. This metaphor describes how a pursuer and a distancer, or partners with different styles of managing anger, advance and retreat and move around one another, having difficulty in finding a comfortable balance between separateness and togetherness.

CHAPTER 10

MANAGING ECONOMIC RESOURCES

CHAPTER OUTLINE

The Stresses of Family Finances
    Finances: A Family Problem
    Finances and Couple Conflict
    Coping with Financial Stressors

Why Do Finances Cause Problems?
    Money: A Taboo Topic
    Common Financial Pitfalls
    The Meaning of Money

Family Income and Expenses
    Family Income
    Annual Household Expenses
    Family Net Worth
    Does It Pay to Work Outside the Home?

Financial Resource Management
    The Process: Stages and Steps
    Budgeting Guidelines
    Pooling Money: Pros and Cons
    Savings

Credit: Uses and Abuses
    Advantages and Disadvantages of Credit
    Purchasing a Home
    Credit Overextension
    Debt and Bankruptcy
    Financial Counseling

LEARNING OBJECTIVES

After reading Chapter 10, you should be able to:

- Discuss why financial issues are the most common problematic issues for couples planning to marry and for families across the family life cycle at all income levels
- Understand how some arguments are not really over money but over power and control in the relationship
- Understand why some families survive economic hard times and why others are torn apart by them
- Summarize some of the coping behaviors and coping strategies people use in difficult economic times
- Discuss why the United States is one of the most affluent nations on earth but still has many people living in poverty
- Discuss the two major stages in the process of managing financial resources
- Discuss why a budget is important and how to create a personal one
- Summarize the basic reasons why people go into debt

PRACTICE TESTS

Key Terms

1. Objectives that an individual or a family want to achieve are _____.
2. _____ involves allocating expenses on a regular basis to ensure there is sufficient money to cover the essentials and a few extras.
3. Being able to survive hard times involves using _____ such as self-esteem and a sense of mastery or confidence in one's ability to learn new skills.
4. _____ is a legal term indicating that a person is financially insolvent and unable to pay her or his debts.
5. What we consider desirable in life and believe is right are our _____.
6. _____, such as cohesion, adaptability, and willingness to adopt nontraditional family roles when economic circumstances change, help a family survive hard times.
7. A(n) _____ has a difficult time avoiding purchasing items for him- or herself and/or others.
8. _____ are what individuals and/or families use to solve problems and reach goals.
9. A(n) _____ is one who keeps very little money on hand for essentials and often purchases the cheapest item, which may be of poor quality and not cost effective in the long run.

Multiple Choice

1. A study of 1,000 families conducted by Olson and his colleagues found that money-related problems are at the highest for families in the _____ stage of the family life cycle.
   a. childbearing
   b. adolescent
   c. launching
   d. retirement

2. According to Mace's survey of 400 physicians and psychiatrists, nearly half believed that _____ is (are) the primary reason that couples quarrel over money.
   a. differences in spouses' spending priorities
   b. differences in spouses' thriftiness
   c. one spouse's using money to dominate and control the other
   d. poor communication

3. Olson and his colleagues found in their study of 1,000 families that _____ is the most stressful financial issue for families across the family life cycle.
   a. money for food, clothing, energy, and home care
   b. purchase of a car or another major item
   c. taking out or refinancing a loan to cover increased expenses
   d. cost of child(ren)'s education

4. What percentage of American families are middle-income?
   a. 22
   b. 33
   c. 44
   d. 55

5. As of 1994, over _____ percent of U.S. children under 18 years of age live in poverty.
   a. 12
   b. 21
   c. 26
   d. 31

6. As of 1994, the average American full-time employed male earned about _____ more per year than the average American full-time employed female.
   a. $2,000
   b. $5,000
   c. $9,000
   d. $12,000

7. Which was NOT brought out in the text as a major factor for the tendency of whites to make more money than African Americans and Hispanics?
   a. People of color live predominantly in urban areas, whereas jobs are moving to the suburbs.
   b. People of color are more likely to work in lower-paying service industries.
   c. Discrimination.
   d. Proportionately there are very few college-educated people of color.

8. The top three (in order) average annual expenditures for urban households in America are:
   a. housing, transportation, food
   b. transportation, housing, clothing
   c. food, health care, housing
   d. housing, health care, food

9. Median income in 1994 of white, African American, and Hispanic households respectively was about:
   a. $30,500, $14,500, $10,000
   b. $45,000, $10,000, $8,000
   c. $62,000, $8,500, $10,000
   d. $39,000, $22,000, $25,000

10. Average income in 1994 of college graduates, high school graduates, and individuals with less than a high school diploma, respectively, was about:
    a. $63,000, $12,500, $7,500
    b. $78,500, $14,000, $8,000
    c. $50,000, $29,000, $13,000
    d. $63,000, $32,000, $15,000

11. By the year 2000, approximately ____ percent of women in the United States will be working outside the home, compared with ____ percent in 1970.
    a. 62; 43
    b. 55; 35
    c. 75; 55
    d. 80; 40

12. How much should a family spend per month of its take-home pay on housing expenses?
    a. one week's
    b. one and a half weeks'
    c. two weeks'
    d. two and a half weeks'

13. Goodman's large-scale survey of American adults found that _____ was the major problem in their families.
    a. children/childrearing issues
    b. sex
    c. household chores/responsibilities
    d. money

14. Which was NOT found by Voydanoff to be a family coping resource influencing how some families cope during hard economic times?
    a. family cohesion
    b. family adaptability
    c. willingness to adopt nontraditional family roles
    d. a sense of mastery in learning new skills to meet changing situations

15. A person with a(n) _____ orientation toward money focuses on the present rather than the future.
    a. status
    b. security
    c. enjoyment
    d. control

True/False

1. Because families tend to spend the increased money they make, there is no significant difference in family stress based on money matters between poor/low-income families and high-income families.
2. According to Blumstein and Schwartz, money matters are the most commonly discussed topic among married couples.
3. According to Arond and Pauker, individuals commonly have both an enjoyment and a security orientation to money.
4. Overall, middle-income families have gained in percentage of money in the United States since the mid-1970s.
5. The median income for families is highest for whites, second highest for African Americans, and third highest for Hispanics.
6. Women with four years of college earn less than men with only a high school diploma.
7. White males receive a higher financial benefit for having a college degree than females and minority groups.
8. Research on couples conducted by Blumstein and Schwartz indicates that two-income couples who favored pooling of their money were more satisfied with money-management issues in their relationship than were those who kept their money separate.
9. In the average urban household, more money is spent each year on alcohol and tobacco than on life insurance.
10. Debt-ridden families come from the lower- and middle-income strata, not from the upper-income level.

Short Answer

1. What are five reasons why finances can cause problems for families?

2. Name Arond and Pauker's four common orientations toward money.

3. What are three reasons for women earning lower incomes than men?

4. Briefly describe the concept of comparable worth, or equal pay for comparable work.

5. What are the four causes of debt, as presented in the text?

Name _____   Chapter 10

PERSONAL INVOLVEMENT ASSESSMENT—
THE WELFARE QUIZ[1]

Taxpayers, members of Congress, state legislators, and individuals actually on welfare agree to some degree that our country's welfare system needs to be fixed. However, there has been a lack of consensus about what Aid to Families with Dependent Children (AFDC) is supposed to be providing and why; how welfare works; and what it does and does not do for the people who receive it. There has been vast disagreement on how to fix the system, Congress and state legislatures have been voting on welfare reform, and welfare reform has been a major campaign issue. Likely, you have certain views on issues concerning welfare. But do you know the facts?

Assessment. Take the Welfare Quiz, found below. Then check the answers on the next page.

1. The AFDC program consumes _____ percent of the federal budget and _____ percent of the average state budget.

2. In 1969, the average number of children in an AFDC family was 3. In 1992, it was _____.

3. _____ percent of AFDC claims are fraudulent.

4. In 1970, 4.1 percent of the population received AFDC; in 1992, at the height of the recession, _____ percent received AFDC.

   a. 9   b. 5.3   c. 1.4   d. 14.2

5. _____ families who receive benefits from AFDC leave the program within one year.

   a. Only a few   b. Almost all   c. More than half   d. About one-fourth

6. The median state AFDC maximum benefit for a family of three in 1994 was _____ a month.

   a. $745   b. $624   c. $254   d. $366

7. In 1994, the median AFDC maximum benefit was _____ percent of the poverty line.

   a. 10   b. 82   c. 36   d. 100

8. After adjusting for inflation, AFDC benefits decreased by _____ percent from 1970 to 1994.

   a. 62   b. 0   c. 45   d. 47

9. In 1991, government tax and transfer systems in Canada lifted about 20 percent of single-parent families out of poverty; in West Germany, about 33 percent; in France, about 50 percent; and in the Netherlands, Sweden, and the United Kingdom, at least 75 percent. In the United States, government tax and transfer systems (AFDC, Food Stamps, etc.) lifted _____ of single-parent families out of poverty.

   a. less than 5 percent   b. 10 percent   c. more than half   d. nearly 40 percent

10. In the 20 years from 1973 to 1993, average weekly inflation-adjusted earnings _____.

    a. declined 19 percent
    b. increased 73 percent
    c. increased 32 percent
    d. increased 14 percent

---

[1] Courtesy of World Hunger Year. *Poverty & Race*, Vol. 4, No. 4, July/August 1995.

Answers: The Welfare Quiz

1. The AFDC program consumes **1 percent** of the federal budget and **2 percent** of the average state budget. (Source: 1994 *Green Book*, U.S. House of Representatives Committee on Ways and Means.)

2. In 1992, the average number of children in an AFDC family was **2**. (Source: 1994 *Green Book*.)

3. **1.4 percent** of AFDC claims are fraudulent. (Source: Quality Control Division, Administration for Children & Families, U.S. Department of Health & Human Services.)

4. **b**. (Source: 1994 *Green Book*.)

5. **c**. (Source: 1994 *Green Book*.)

6. **d**. (Source: 1994 *Green Book*.)

7. **c**. (Source: 1994 *Green Book*.)

8. **d**. (Source: 1994 *Green Book*.)

9. **a**. (Source: Tufts University Center on Hunger, Poverty & Nutrition Policy, *Citing* Joint Center for Political & Economic Studies.)

10. **a**. (Source: Tufts University Center on Hunger, Poverty & Nutrition Policy, *Citing* Bureau of Labor Statistics, U.S. Department of Labor.)

Now, write about how your responses compared to the correct answers.

What, if anything, surprised you about the information?

What are your views on welfare?

Name _____   Chapter 10

KNOWLEDGE IN ACTION—
IMAGE OF THE "SUCCESSFUL FAMILY" IN ADVERTISING

Most, if not all, Americans are exposed to the media on a daily basis, whether they view television, listen to the radio, or read newspapers and magazines. Although each medium is unique in the way it advertises products to pay for its operations, all media—except for those that are public-supported—are reliant on sponsors of some sort. And the sponsors, diverse as they may be, are all interested in selling their products. The key thing is to figure out the best ways to get the public to buy their products. Thus, they are likely to hire advertising firms and marketing experts to help in devising the most productive strategies.

Successful advertising campaigns are those that provide an appeal to prospective buyers. Certainly, in a society based on capitalism and monetary success, advertising images of financial success, personal success, self-worth, self-assurance, etc., are those that have appeal. And, as such, the ads need to sell more than just the product; they need to sell how the buyer will *feel* owning, or wearing, or driving, or being seen with the product. Image is important in the American society—the image we project to others as well as the image we have of ourselves.

Project. For this exercise, select one type of media and conduct a *content analysis* of advertised products that pertain to families and their economic resources. For example, watch television, noticing the ways in which families, husbands, and/or wives are portrayed in commercials—in the home, in paying bills, at a bank, giving allowances to their children, etc. Or look over ads found in several magazines. Develop ahead of time a list of items to check. Tally the relative numbers found and jot down some of the more noteworthy examples. If you are using magazine ads, cut some out and attach to this exercise. Analyze and summarize your findings.

Media Used.

Tally.

Results.

Discussion.

(Attach another sheet of paper if needed.)

ANSWER KEY

Key Terms

1. goals
2. Budgeting
3. personal coping resources
4. Bankruptcy
5. values
6. Family coping resources
7. spender
8. Resources
9. saver

Multiple Choice

1. b
2. c
3. a
4. d
5. b
6. d
7. d
8. a
9. d
10. c
11. a
12. a
13. d
14. d
15. c

True/False

1. F
2. T
3. F
4. F
5. F
6. T
7. T
8. F
9. T
10. F

Suggested Responses to Short Answer Questions

1. 1) Money is a taboo topic in many families; 2) couples tend to have unrealistic expectations about finances; 3) many couples do not develop and adhere to a budget; 4) some families overspend and rely too heavily on credit; 5) partners have different styles of spending and saving; 6) partners differ as to the meaning of money; 7) one partner uses money as a tool to gain power and control over the other partner.

2. Money as status, money as security, money as enjoyment, and money as control over one's life.

3. 1) Women often drop out of the labor force to care for children at home; 2) men gain seniority over women in the labor force; 3) women have little legal recourse today when paid lower wages for the same jobs or for jobs that require comparable skills; 4) jobs traditionally held by women tend to command lower salaries.

4. Workers are paid based on the number of years of education, training, and experience the job demands, as well as on the comparative difficulty of the job in contrast with other jobs. This approach attempts to correct the inequities based on traditional gender-role assumptions.

5. 1) Credit spending, 2) crisis spending, 3) careless or impulsive spending, 4) compulsive spending.

CHAPTER 11

COHABITATION, MARRIAGE, AND EARLY MARRIED LIFE

CHAPTER OUTLINE

Cohabitation
    Cohabitation As Preparation for Marriage
    Cohabiting and Relationship Satisfaction
    Cohabiting As a Courtship Stage
    Cohabiting and Relationship Longevity
    Legal Issues in Cohabitation
    Same-Sex Cohabitation
    Questions to Consider Before Cohabiting

Formula for a Successful Marriage

Reasons for Marrying
    Positive Reasons
    Negative Reasons

Parental Perspective and Influence on Marriage

Preparing for Marriage
    Can Couples Prepare for Marriage?
    How Effective Are Premarital Programs?
    What Constitutes an Effective Premarital Program?
    Predicting a Successful Marriage with PREPARE

Using the Family Circumplex Model in Premarital Counseling
    A Structurally Enmeshed Family of Origin
    A Flexibly Disengaged Family of Origin
    Goals for the Relationship

From the Wedding Through the Early Married Years
    The Wedding
    Newlyweds: The Difficult Adjustment
    The Early Years of Marriage: Issues and Strengths
    Some Recommendations for a Happy Marriage

LEARNING OBJECTIVES

After reading Chapter 11, you should be able to:
- Discuss the four major types of cohabitation and the dynamics behind each
- Outline important questions to ask oneself before cohabiting
- List and explain the conditions that give a marriage a better chance of survival
- Discuss positive reasons and negative reasons for getting married
- Discuss why it is important to spend time preparing for marriage and why it is important to expose the differences between partners before marriage
- Discuss the significance of the statement "You don't marry an individual, you marry a whole family"
- Summarize why the first year or two of marriage are the most difficult for most couples, and list some useful tips for making the adjustment less stressful
- List some of the major stressors newlywed couples have to deal with and some coping techniques couples use or develop to deal with these stressors

PRACTICE TESTS

Key Terms

1. Two unrelated adults engage in _____ when they share the same living quarters and have an emotional and sexual relationship.
2. The _____ type of cohabitation involves one partner being so dependent and insecure that cohabiting with anyone is preferable to being alone.
3. Living with someone else in order to break away from parental values and influence is the _____ type of cohabitation.
4. _____ cohabitation usually is begun by a man wanting someone living with him to supply sex, loving care, and domestic labor; the woman usually does not share the same motivation.
5. Treating cohabitation as a trial for marriage is the _____ type of cohabitation.
6. A premarital inventory used in assessing areas of an engaged couple's relationship is known as _____.
7. Equitable relief awarded to an unmarried partner following an unsuccessful cohabitation is referred to as _____.
8. _____ are those in which partners were brought up during childhood.

Multiple Choice

1. Which of the following is the best single predictor of marital success?
    a. socioeconomic status
    b. length of courtship
    c. age at marriage
    d. complementary personalities

2. The law of enlightened self-interest is reflected in:
    a. one partner trying to get his/her own way all the time
    b. assertive communication
    c. loving oneself in order to love another
    d. focusing on one's lover's needs, with the lover reciprocating

3. Between 1980 and 1993, the number of couples cohabiting _____.
    a. doubled
    b. tripled
    c. quadrupled
    d. remained roughly the same

4. Which type of premarital counseling technique has been found to be superior over the others?
    a. traditional discussion sessions with clergy
    b. group lectures
    c. premarital inventory
    d. none superior to the others

5. Using the PREPARE inventory with engaged couples prior to marriage, researchers have found a _____ percent accuracy rate in predicting whether a couple would be happily married or divorced, three to four years after marrying.
    a. 25 to 30
    b. 45 to 50
    c. 60 to 65
    d. 80 to 85

6. Which of these common patterns of cohabitation, as identified by Ridley, Peterman, and Avery, often has the relationship end with one partner's feeling guilty?
   a. Linus blanket
   b. emancipation
   c. convenience
   d. testing

7. A survey conducted by Korbel and Brothers of 1,000 couples soon to be married found that over _____ percent of the individuals questioned whether they were making the right decision.
   a. 25
   b. 40
   c. 65
   d. 80

8. Arond and Pauker's survey of 455 newlyweds and 75 couples married a few years found that about _____ doubted their marriage would last during their first year of marriage.
   a. one-fourth
   b. one-half
   c. two-thirds
   d. three-fourths

9. Stewart and Olson's research with over 5,000 premarital couples indicated all EXCEPT which of the following?
   a. A very high percentage of the engaged couples with both sets of parents feeling negative about the upcoming marriage reported low premarital satisfaction.
   b. About half of the engaged couples with both sets of parents feeling positive about the upcoming marriage reported positive premarital satisfaction.
   c. About three-fourths of the engaged couples with one set of parents feeling negative about the upcoming marriage reported low premarital satisfaction.
   d. No correlation was found between parental support of the upcoming marriage and level of couples' premarital satisfaction.

10. According to Stewart and Olson, engaged couples having the highest level of premarital satisfaction are those who:
    a. both live alone
    b. live with parents or others
    c. both live with parents
    d. cohabit

11. Which characteristic(s) did Fowers and Olson find to be the MOST important predictor of a happy marriage for couples taking the PREPARE premarital inventory?
    a. financial management
    b. children/parenting
    c. relationship
    d. having realistic expectations

12. What new term was coined as a result of the *Marvin* v. *Marvin* cohabitation lawsuit?
    a. contract cohabitation
    b. convenience cohabitation
    c. palimony
    d. cohabital alimony

13. Which type of cohabitation often involves an "invisible" relationship?
    a. convenience
    b. same-sex
    c. Linus blanket
    d. none of the above

14. Which of the following was found by Stewart and Olson to have the greatest influence on engaged couples' premarital satisfaction?
    a. both sets of parents feeling negative about the upcoming marriage
    b. both sets of parents feeling positive about the upcoming marriage
    c. both sets of parents being married
    d. both sets of parents being divorced

15. According to Arond and Pauker, newlyweds experience which of the following as the greatest challenge in their marriage?
    a. marital problems relating to money
    b. sexual problems
    c. their mate becoming more critical of them
    d. maintaining relationships with single friends

True/False

1. Watson's study of married Canadian couples indicated that cohabiters were better adjusted to marriage than noncohabitors during their first year of marriage.
2. Parents' marital status has not been found to have a significant influence on premarital satisfaction of the engaged couple.
3. Premarital education programs utilizing large group-lecture formats have been found to be effective in producing attitude change.
4. Research indicates a very low rate of predictability for success of marriage using the PREPARE Inventory before marriage.
5. According to research conducted by Arond and Pauker of newlyweds and couples married a few years, couples who lived together before marriage had significantly lower marital satisfaction scores than those who had not lived together before marriage.
6. Undesirable traits in a person before marriage tend to diminish during marriage.
7. Stewart and Olson found in their large study of engaged couples that cohabiting couples had lower levels of premarital satisfaction than did couples living apart.
8. Attending premarital large-group lectures increases the likelihood that a couple will see a marriage counselor if they experience marital problems.
9. Love is the most important factor in predicting the success of a marriage.
10. The adage "When you get married, you marry a whole family" is relevant today.

Short Answer

1. What have been found to be the main differences between traditional courtship and cohabitation as preparation for marriage, according to critics of traditional courtship as well as critics of cohabitation?

2. What are three negative reasons for getting married?

3. What are the components found to be essential to an effective premarital program?

4. What are the five recommendations offered by Arond and Pauker to newlywed couples?

5. What did Olson and his colleagues find to be the major stressors for young married couples?

Name _____   Chapter 11

PERSONAL INVOLVEMENT ASSESSMENT—
SAME-SEX MARRIAGE

A section in the text, "Same-Sex Cohabitation," brings out the societal stigmatization felt by same-sex cohabitants as well as concerns over their lack of legal status and discomfort about their sexual orientation felt by family members and friends. Because of these difficulties, many do not reveal their sexual preference publicly, even though they may be totally committed to their long-term relationship.

Marriage, to heterosexuals as well as gays and lesbians, means commitment, but also societal validation accorded to married couples. Partly to be able to acquire that validation, three couples challenged Hawaii's law prohibiting same-sex marriages. Their challenge was upheld by the Hawaii Supreme Court, which will be making another ruling soon. However, even if the state court overturns Hawaii's law, the U.S. Congress has enacted a law allowing states to refuse to recognize same-sex marriages performed in other states. The new law defines marriage as a union between a man and a woman only.

What are same-sex couples *not* able to have by not being able to be married? In addition to marriage validating married couples, it provides many rights that same-sex couples do not present have but would like to have. Some examples include being able to:

- help make critical-care decisions for their spouse in hospitals
- be protected from having to testify in court against their spouse
- sue for loss of companionship if their spouse is injured or killed through negligence
- be included in their spouse's health insurance plan
- upon their spouse's death, have the rights to inheritance and pension benefits and a presumed right to continue custody of adopted or birth children and make burial decisions
- in case of divorce, be protected if one is the less financially powerful spouse

Assessment. What do you think should or should not be available to gay and lesbian couples in the way of rights?

Should gay and lesbian couples be able to marry? Why? Why not? If not, should they be entitled to the same benefits as married couples?

Should same-sex couples who are legally able to marry in one state have their marriages recognized in other states? Why? Why not?

Specifically, what benefits do you believe should or should not be available?

- help make critical-care decisions for their spouse in hospital
- be protected from having to testify in court against their spouse
- sue for loss of companionship if their spouse is injured or killed through negligence
- be included in their spouse's health insurance plan
- when their spouse dies, have the rights to inheritance and pension benefits and a presumed right to continue custody of adopted or birth children and to make burial decisions
- in case of divorce, be protected if one is the less financially powerful spouse
- other?

Overall, what are your thoughts on same-sex cohabitation?

On same-sex marriage?

If same-sex marriages are not legally available to gay and lesbian couples, should there be legal provisions available for them to receive the same benefits that married couples have?

Name _____ Chapter 11

KNOWLEDGE IN ACTION—
COHABITATION AND MARITAL STABILITY

Does "living together," or cohabiting, prior to marriage make a difference in how committed the couple is as well as in the chance of divorce later on? You probably can find many people who would say yes as well as many people who would say no.

Elizabeth Thomson and Ugo Colella investigated these and other views using data from more than 13,000 adults sampled as part of the 1987–88 National Survey of Families and Households. They limited their analysis to couples in their first marriages who had never cohabited with anyone else. In addition, all couples had been married less than 10 years.

Generally, the couples who had cohabited prior to marriage (in contrast to couples who had not cohabited prior to marriage) reported lower-quality marriages, less commitment to the institution of marriage, and greater likelihood of divorce. Thomson and Colella found that the length of cohabitation increased the effects. Looking at three categories of likelihood of divorce, *low, very low,* and *even or higher,* the researchers found differences between those who did not cohabit and those who did, as evidenced in the following table:

Table 1. Perceived Likelihood of Divorce by Cohabitation Experience

Likelihood of Divorce	Did Not Cohabit	Months Cohabited			
		1–5	6–11	12–23	24+
Very low	61.2%	50.9%	49.6%	36.0%	38.8%
Low	27.0	28.2	29.6	48.2	39.2
Even or higher	11.8	20.9	20.8	15.8	22.0

As can be seen in the findings presented in Table 1, couples who cohabited before marriage were more likely to accept the possibility of divorce than were couples who had not cohabited. Also, the longer a couple had cohabited, the more likely they were to perceive the possibility of divorce.

Project. Select one of the following two options for interviewing people about the topic of cohabitation and marital stability.

Option 1: Cohabiting and Noncohabiting Couples. Interview several married couples, some who cohabited prior to marriage and some who did not. Develop questions ahead of time pertaining to quality of their marriage, commitment to the institution of marriage, and likelihood of their getting divorced. You may want to interview the partners separately. Analyze your findings with regard to whether the couples' having cohabited or not makes a difference in these three areas.

Option 2: Attitudes About Cohabitation and Marital Stability. Interview several college students about their attitudes toward cohabitation and whether this would have an effect on future marital stability. Develop questions ahead of time pertaining to their attitudes on cohabitation and whether they believe cohabitation would influence quality of a couple's marriage, commitment to the institution of marriage, and likelihood of their getting divorced. Contrast your findings to those in the national survey.

Table 1: Elizabeth Thomson and Ugo Colella, "Cohabitation and Marital Stability: Quality or Commitment?" *Journal of Marriage and the Family* 54 (May 1992): 259–267. Copyright © 1992 by the National Council on Family Relations, 3989 Central Ave., NE, Suite 550, Minneapolis, MN 55421. Reprinted by permission.

Sample.

Results.

Discussion/Analysis.

ANSWER KEY

Key Terms

1. cohabitation
2. Linus blanket
3. emancipation
4. Convenience
5. testing
6. PREPARE
7. palimony
8. Families of origin

Multiple Choice

1. c	6. a	11. c
2. d	7. c	12. c
3. a	8. b	13. b
4. c	9. d	14. a
5. d	10. a	15. a

True/False

1. F	6. F
2. F	7. T
3. F	8. F
4. F	9. F
5. T	10. T

Suggested Responses to Short Answer Questions

1. Critics of traditional courtship: traditional courtship emphasizes recreation and avoids conflictual issues and solving problems. It provides partners with idealized views of each other, whereas cohabiting partners are able to experience the realities of life together before deciding to marry. Critics of cohabitation: cohabitation is inherently immoral and violates religious dogma. It is only "playing house."

2. 1) Premarital pregnancy, 2) rebellion against parents, 3) independence, 4) rebounding from another relationship, 5) family or social pressure, 6) economic security.

3. 1) The couple should take some type of premarital inventory and should receive feedback on the results; 2) the couple should participate in a small discussion group in which couples share their feelings; 3) the couple should receive training in communication and problem-solving skills.

4. 1) Acknowledge and handle hostility, 2) tolerate imperfections and differences, 3) separate from your families of origin, 4) be committed, and 5) realize that marriage has its ups and downs.

5. Issues relating to work and family, finances, relationships, and illness.

CHAPTER 12

PARENTHOOD

CHAPTER OUTLINE

The Challenge of Parenthood
    Conventional Wisdom About Parenting
    The Transition to Parenthood
    Financial Issues and Children
    Adoption: Moving Toward Openness

Parenting and the Family Circumplex Model
    Styles of Parenting
    Parenting Styles and the Circumplex Model
    The Effects of Children on the Family Across the Family Life Cycle

Issues in Parenting
    Practical Approaches to Childrearing
    Increasing Use of Day Care
    Coparenting
    Fatherhood Today
    Parent Education and Family Therapy
    Challenges and Pleasures of Parenthood

LEARNING OBJECTIVES

After reading Chapter 12, you should be able to:

- Discuss why parenthood can be the most challenging yet satisfying job one can ever have
- Summarize some of the popular folk beliefs about parenthood
- Discuss the phrase "parenthood as crisis"
- Summarize how those who are voluntarily childless can find as much satisfaction in a life as those who have children
- Understand the financial issues of raising children
- Discuss parenting styles and the Family Circumplex Model, including some philosophical questions about childrearing

PRACTICE TESTS

Key Terms

1. The _____ approach involves cooperation and an equal sharing of responsibilities for child care, housework, and work outside the home.

2. The _____ of child development focuses on the importance of body areas for children as they develop and of providing a positive emotional environment for the child.

3. Parents meeting in group settings and engaged in group discussion of general parenting problems are involved with _____.

4. Nonparenthood, voluntary childlessness, and the _____ are all terms applying to the choice not to have children.

5. Baumrind's style of parenting that is democratic, involving setting of clear rules and expectations for the child's behavior, is the _____ style.

6. The taking on of tasks traditionally associated with both female and male roles in parenting reflects a(n) _____ style.

7. The _____ style can bring about children who are loners, withdrawn, and low achievers.

8. That style of parenting in which parents set rigid rules and expectations, demanding obedience, is _____.

9. Consensus developed in the 1980s among child-development researchers about the need to study _____ in parent-child dynamics—the effects of the child on the parent and those of the parent on the child.

10.–12. Proponents of _____ of child development, including those considering themselves _____, emphasize the importance of _____ of positive behavior.

13. The _____ style provides little attention to a child's needs, often producing immature children with psychological problems.

14. The _____ of child development focuses on cognitive development and thought processes.

15. A single family working on one or more specific family problems with a therapist is involved with _____.

16. _____ enables the child's preferences to take priority over the parents' ideals with no or little forcing of the child to conform to the parents' standards.

Multiple Choice

1. About ____ percent of all females in the United States give birth to a baby before their 20th birthday.
   a. 13
   b. 20
   c. 25
   d. 27

2. Research conducted by LeMasters back in the 1950s was the first to look at the coming of a child as a "crisis" for a married couple. LeMasters found that over _____ percent of the 46 couples interviewed defined their situation in this way.
   a. 25
   b. 40
   c. 60
   d. 80

3. According to 1994 U.S. Bureau of the Census figures, ____ percent of American wives between the ages of 18 and 34 do NOT expect to have children.
   a. 9
   b. 15
   c. 25
   d. 30

4. Which was NOT cited in the text from a review of the literature on research conducted on voluntary childlessness?
   a. Older adults without children do quite well without children and/or grandchildren.
   b. Nonparents overall exhibit more psychological problems than parents.
   c. A disproportionate number of women of eminence are childless.
   d. Child-free couples tend to have more vital and happy relationships than do couples with children.

5. Middle-income families (earning between $29,900 and $48,300 yearly) spend an estimated _____ on rearing each child from birth to 17:
   a. $75,000
   b. $90,000
   c. $120,000
   d. $168,000

6. A strong consensus developed among traditional child-development researchers in the _____ about the need to study bidirectional effects on parent-child dynamics.
   a. 1960s
   b. 1970s
   c. 1980s
   d. 1990s

7. According to Baumrind, children of _____ parents tend to be moody, vulnerable to stress, and often unfriendly.
   a. authoritative
   b. authoritarian
   c. permissive
   d. rejecting

8. Baumrind found that children of _____ parents tend to be rebellious, domineering, and low achievers.
   a. authoritative
   b. authoritarian
   c. permissive
   d. rejecting

9. The _____ style of parenting falls into the balanced area of the Circumplex Model.
   a. authoritative
   b. authoritarian
   c. permissive
   d. rejecting

10. Which style of parenting tends to be low in both cohesion (disengaged) and flexibility (rigid)?
    a. authoritative
    b. authoritarian
    c. permissive
    d. rejecting

11. Which type of couple did Olson and his colleagues find to have the highest level of family cohesion?
    a. young couples without children
    b. childbearing couples
    c. couples with adolescents
    d. launching couples

12. Which has NOT been found by researchers to be an advantage of the coparenting model?
    a. It frees women to pursue interests outside the home.
    b. It facilitates greater satisfaction of the parents with their marriage and family life.
    c. It helps men to learn how to be attentive to the emotional needs of others.
    d. It allows parents more time to focus on their marriage and relationship.

13. Which parenting style is favored currently?
    a. authoritative
    b. authoritarian
    c. permissive
    d. rejecting

14. The uninvolved style of parenting often is combined with Baumrind's _____ style of parenting.
    a. authoritative
    b. authoritarian
    c. permissive
    d. rejecting

15. Which parenting model focuses on the cognitive development of children and adolescents?
    a. psychodynamic
    b. organismic
    c. behaviorist
    d. coparenting

True/False

1. Research indicates that children always turn out fine as adults as long as they have good, loving parents.
2. A child's temperament is learned, not present at birth.
3. According to research findings, there are both advantages and disadvantages to having only one child.
4. Contrary to what many people believe, sex education in the schools does NOT stimulate interest in sex and create more sexual problems.
5. A stable one-parent family household is better for a child than an unstable two-parent household.
6. The "empty-nest syndrome" has been found to plague most parents in middle years.
7. Couples WITHOUT children tend to be more flexible and more cohesive than couples with children.
8. Adults with problems tend to have had problems as children.
9. Organismic theorists encourage parents to select toys and activities that are at an appropriate developmental level for their children.
10. Parenting utilizing a behaviorist approach focuses on strict and consistent discipline, regardless of the circumstances.

Short Answer

1. Identify and briefly describe Baumrind's four parenting styles.

2. Describe the four approaches to parenting discussed in the text.

3. Contrast parent education and family therapy.

4. Why doesn't parenting require special training or education as do other jobs in our society?

5. Identify ten myths about parenting that were discussed in the text.

Name _____   Chapter 12

PERSONAL INVOLVEMENT ASSESSMENT—
FATHERS AND SONS

In a *Psychology Today* essay, "Fathers & Sons: What It Takes to Be a Man," the concept of fatherhood is discussed—specifically, how it has changed so completely over the past 200 years. Whereas at one time masculinity was defined in terms of skills at fathering and husbanding, it increasingly has become defined in terms of making money and providing for the family.

Psychology Today editors wonder if the current crop of fathers will fare better. They believe that what goes on between a father and a son is critical for determining whether the son will become a man who is capable of emotional intimacy with other men, women, and children. To them, hands-on fathering is essential for men to heal and for boys to grow up to want to be fathers, not just providers for their families.

Assessment. Read over the following types of fathers from the *Psychology Today* essay. Then briefly describe how your father or father figure fit this description. Make accommodations to this exercise if you had no father or father figure, if you are presently a father yourself, if you are a woman, etc.

* <u>Father the Provider</u>: . . . bringing things home to the family rather than living and working at home *within* the family. . . . The father's position in the family was no longer determined by how well he functioned as a father, but was scored by his status in the eyes of the world, in a set of economic contests in which there were few men winning by being the richest of them all, and most men losing. . . .

    He didn't slow down when he'd achieved a level of sufficient comfort; instead, he strove even harder to get the approval of his fellow workers and to earn glory in their eyes. He worked because he worked; that was what he did because that was what he was. . . . In the endeavors and identity dearest to his heart and heaviest on his schedule, he was a working man, and his family should understand that their claims on his time came second at best.

    Your father (father figure):

* <u>Father the Success</u>: When society decided that raising children was women's work and that making money was the single-minded point of men's lives, fathers became too busy for their children and boys began to grow up without fathers. That would not have been critical if there were uncles and cousins and grandfathers and older brothers around to model masculinity for boys. But our ideas of mental health and the goals of the housing industry required that families tie themselves down to the size of a married couple and their children.

    Reducing the family to such a tiny, isolated, nuclear unit made it mobile enough for the purposes of industrial society. . . . Now nothing came between a man and his job. . . . Men on the Daddy Track were severely penalized, much as women on the Mommy Track are now.

    The children of this generation may grow up with the idea that a father's life is his work, and his family should not expect anything more from him.

    Your father (father figure):

Source of this section is "Fathers & Sons: What It Takes to Be a Man," *Psychology Today*, September/October 1993, pp. 52–54.

* <u>Father Hunger</u>: Life for most boys and for many grown men then is a frustrating search for the lost father who has not yet offered protection, provision, nurturing, modeling, or, especially, anointment. All those tough guys who want to scare the world into seeing them as men and who fill up the jails; all those men who don't know how to be a man with a woman and who fill up the divorce courts; all those corporate raiders who want more in hopes that more will make them feel better . . . —all of them are suffering from Father Hunger.

> They go through their adolescent rituals day after day for a lifetime, waiting for a father to anoint them and treat them as good enough to be considered a man.
>
> They call attention to their pain, getting into trouble, getting hurt, doing things that are bad for them, as if they are calling for a father to come take them in hand and straighten them out or at least tell them how a grown man would handle the pain.
>
> They compete with other boys but don't get close enough to let them see their shame over not feeling like men, over not having been anointed, and so they don't know that the other boys feel the same way.

Your father (father figure):

* <u>Father the Nurturer</u>: Fathering makes a man—whatever his standing in the eyes of the world—feel strong and good and important, just as he makes his child feel loved and valued.

> . . . A father who gets to hang out with his children is reliving the joys of his own childhood. The play is the thing.
>
> Becoming Father the Nurturer rather than just Father the Provider enables a man to fully feel and express his humanity and masculinity. Fathering is the most masculine thing a man can do.

Your father (father figure):

Name _____   Chapter 12

KNOWLEDGE IN ACTION—
GUILT OF WORKING MOTHERS

The media have given much attention to the working mother and whether she should be on the "mommy track" or the "career track." Of course, fathers work as well, but the American working mother (working outside the home in addition to working in the home) rather than the working father is the one who appears to feel the more strongly about her responsibilities with the children and to feel guilty about not spending enough time with the children as well as enough time on the job.

Barbara Berg, a historian and self-described guilt-ridden mother, writes of her own personal feelings of guilt over being an inadequate mother and an inadequate career professional and of the guilt expressed by nearly 1,000 women of varying backgrounds whom she interviewed.[1] She found a great deal of self-reproach—for going back to work, for taking a leave of absence, for leaving the office early, for working late, for not being with the children, and so on. Guilt affected the women's work (staying in low-level jobs), their home life (being martyrs about doing more than their share of the housework yet undermining their husband's efforts at helping out and losing sexual spontaneity), their personal life (neglecting their physical and emotional health), and their relationships with their children (being too indulgent with their children).

Overall, according to Berg, what today's working mother forgets is that American mothers have always worked and that they should not feel guilty about doing so! They should be praised for their efforts instead of being condemned for being selfish. They should become angry about the lack of child-care support by corporations and the government rather than misdirecting their anger at their spouses, children, and themselves. And, Berg writes, they should join together with other working mothers and fathers for support and to work for changes in corporate and public policies that would be sensitive to the needs of families. Then, and only then, will working mothers be freed from the "tyranny of guilt."

Project. Prepare questions to use in interviewing one or two working mothers—preferably at least one of whom is involved in a career. It might also be interesting to include a single parent. Develop questions ahead of time pertaining to strain and conflict experienced in attempting to juggle career with parenthood and marriage. Summarize your findings and contrast them with those presented about Berg's research and in the chapter.

Questions Asked.

---

[1] Barbara Berg, "The Guilt That Drives Working Mothers Crazy," *Ms.*, May 1987, 56–59, 73–74.

Summary of Findings.

Implications.

ANSWER KEY

Key Terms

1. coparenting
2. psychodynamic theory
3. parent education
4. child-free alternative
5. authoritative parenting
6. coparenting
7. uninvolved parenting
8. authoritarian parenting
9. bidirectional effects
10. learning theories
11. behaviorist
12. reinforcement
13. rejecting parenting
14. organismic theory
15. family therapy
16. Permissive parenting

Multiple Choice

1. a
2. d
3. a
4. b
5. c
6. c
7. b
8. c
9. a
10. d
11. a
12. d
13. a
14. d
15. b

True/False

1. F
2. F
3. T
4. T
5. T
6. F
7. T
8. T
9. T
10. F

Suggested Responses to Short Answer Questions

1. 1) Authoritative (democratic): parents establish clear rules and expectations that are discussed with the child, using both reason and power to enforce their standards; 2) authoritarian: parents establish and enforce rigid rules and expectations, demanding obedience; 3) permissive: parents let child's preferences take priority over their ideals, rarely forcing child to conform to their standards; 4) rejecting: parents pay little attention to child's needs and seldom have expectations about the child's behavior; 5) uninvolved (often combined with the rejecting style): parents often ignore the child, letting child's preferences prevail if they do not interfere with parents' activities.

2. 1) Psychodynamic: focus on psychological and personality development, adhered to by Freudians and others who stress the importance of providing a positive emotional environment for the child and stages of physical development of the child; 2) organismic: focus on cognitive development, adhered to by Piaget and others, stressing the developing of the mind through various stages throughout childhood and adolescence; 3) behaviorist: focus on learning and reinforcement of positives through rewards; 4) coparenting: focus on shared parenting—the parents' sharing of traditional parental and work roles.

3. Parent education involves a presentation of information followed by a group discussion of common parenting problems. Family therapy involves a therapist working with a single family with one or more specific problems.

4. We tend to leave family matters private, not wanting to interfere with a family's right to bring up their children as they wish.

5. 1) Rearing children is fun, 2) children are sweet and cute, 3) children will turn out well if they have "good" parents, 4) children improve a marriage, 5) good parents can manage any child, no matter what the child's nature, 6) today's parents are not as good as yesterday's, 7) couples without children are frustrated and unhappy, 8) one child is too few, 9) there are no bad children—only bad parents, 10) all parents are adults, 11) children appreciate the sacrifices their parents make and the advantages they provide, 12) sex education creates more sexual behavior, 13) parenthood receives top priority in our society, 14) love is enough to guarantee good parental performance, 15) one-parent families are problematic, 16) parenting ends when the children leave home, 17) the "empty-nest syndrome" leaves many parents lonely and depressed, and 18) parents alone should rear the young.

CHAPTER 13

MIDLIFE AND OLDER COUPLES

CHAPTER OUTLINE

Family Life in the Middle Years
    Defining Middle Age
    The Middle-Aged Person and the Working World
    Sexuality in Middle Age
    The Middle-Aged Marriage
    Empty Nest or Spacious Nest?
    Caught in the Middle: The Sandwich Generation
    Grandparenthood

Family Life in the Later Years
    Defining Old Age
    Conventional Wisdom About Old Age
    Retirement
    Family Dynamics and the Aging Couple
    Losing a Spouse

LEARNING OBJECTIVES

After reading Chapter 13, you should be able to:

- Discuss middle age, the phrase "Life begins at 40," and the term *middlescent*
- Summarize why the biggest challenge to men in midlife is how to thrive in the working world while maintaining a successful family life
- Discuss the effects of middle age on women
- Discuss middle-age sexuality, including menopause and "male menopause"
- List some warning signs of problems in middle-age marriages
- Summarize some recommendations for strengthening marriage in the middle years
- Understand the difference between an empty nest and a spacious nest
- Discuss some other concerns of middle-age marriages: boomerang kids, sandwich generation, and grandparenthood
- Outline the myths about old age and retirement
- Define *old age* using Neugarten's divisions
- Discuss some concerns of long-term marriages
- Understand how the death of a spouse is a difficult life transition for most people, what aspects of grief people are likely to experience, and important elements of successfully coping with this loss

PRACTICE TESTS

Key Terms

1. The period of adjustment that is viewed positively by the parents—giving them more room, time, and money—once their children leave home is the _____.
2. Production of the male hormone _____ decreases in middle-aged men.
3. The _____ is the first stage in the grieving process and involves a state of shock for the survivor of the loss.
4. The years between roughly 35 to 40 and 65 for many people, and encompassing the family stages of teenagers to launching young adults, is generally known as _____.
5. Many parents are now finding themselves _____, taking care of children as well as their aging parents, thus becoming part of the "sandwich generation."
6. The _____ is the last of the three stages of the grieving process and involves a change in lifestyle for the survivor without the deceased partner.
7. The _____ involves a period of adjustment for parents when their children are launched away from the home, causing problems for some parents but a more positive situation for others.
8. A parent is of the _____ when taking care of both children and aging parents at home.
9. Prejudice against older people is _____.
10. Adult children returning home for help from their parents is a _____.
11. The second stage of the grieving process is the _____, in which the survivor tries to create a new life.
12. _____ on the job, involving the job's becoming so comfortable that there's no longer any challenge in it, can contribute to middle-age crisis.
13. Usually thought to begin at age 65 or at the age of retirement, _____ may be more accurately described as a psychological phenomenon having to do with how one feels about growing older.
14. _____ involves emotional and physical changes in some men caused by lessening of the production of androgen.
15. Marriages lasting 50 years or more are _____.
16. The end of the monthly menstrual cycle for women is known as _____.
17. A(n) _____ can occur during one's middle years, especially if one is not motivated at work or in one's marriage.
18. _____ are adult children who return home following divorce, job loss, or inability to make it in the real world.

Multiple Choice

1. A parent experiences the _____ when caring for both children and aging parents.
    a. boomerang nest
    b. sandwich generation
    c. cluttered nest
    d. nurture syndrome
2. The greatest challenge in midlife—especially for men—has to do with their:
    a. family life
    b. sexuality
    c. work/careers
    d. health

3. Female menopause begins on the average at about the age of ____.
   a. 40
   b. 45
   c. 50
   d. 55

4. Hayes's early research on divorce in the middle years found which two major reasons for the marriages having survived for so long before divorce?
   a. children and money
   b. communication and sex
   c. money and sex
   d. job problems and money

5. Which of the following statements was NOT found to be the case in most of the middle-year divorces in Hayes's early study?
   a. Most individuals said their partner did not contribute to feelings of self-esteem.
   b. Both partners often referred to their marriage as boring.
   c. Extramarital affairs were as common among the men as among the women.
   d. Husbands were frequently reported as having become obsessed with their appearance.

6. Which of the following is NOT one of the three categories of longevis marriages discussed by Rowe and Lasswell?
   a. unstable couples, swinging back and forth between being happy and unhappy
   b. happy couples, blissfully in love
   c. unhappy couples who stay married out of habit or fear
   d. in-between couples, neither very happy nor very unhappy

7. About one in ____ of all the 18- to 34-year-olds in the country are living with their parents.
   a. four
   b. five
   c. six
   d. ten

8. What percentage of persons aged 65 or older have living grandchildren?
   a. 90
   b. 75
   c. 60
   d. 50

9. The average life expectancy in the United States is about ____ years.
   a. 65
   b. 70
   c. 75
   d. 80

10. Brubaker's review of research conducted on older couples' relationships supports which of the following generalizations?
    a. The quality of the marital relationship maintains continuity throughout the years.
    b. Most relationships decline in marital quality over the years.
    c. Most relationships improve over the years.
    d. No patterns were found to a significant degree to warrant making any generalizations.

11. The average life expectancy of women is about ____ years more than that of men.
    a. 3
    b. 5
    c. 7
    d. 9

12. Which is NOT a myth about old age?
    a. Most old people lose their sex drive.
    b. Most old people are more likely to wind up being cared for by their families than in nursing homes.
    c. Most old people are lonely.
    d. Most old people are poor.

13. According to Brubaker, which stage of the grieving process following the death of a spouse is characterized by the widow or widower developing an identity without the partner?
    a. crisis-loss
    b. transition
    c. new life
    d. none of the above

14. _____ wives can expect to become widows.
    a. One in four
    b. Half of all
    c. Two-thirds of all
    d. Three-fourths of all

15. Which term refers to the situation in which adult children return home to live for a while, usually to save money to move into their own apartments or homes?
    a. empty nest syndrome
    b. cluttered nest
    c. boomerang nest
    d. nurture nest

True/False

1. "Male menopause" is often referred to as the silent passage.

2. Perceptions of pleasure and satisfaction in sexual intercourse decline for women in menopause.

3. Hayes's early study of divorce in the middle years found that in most of the marriages one of the major problems was with the husband's being overly dominant.

4. "Cluttered nests" are less likely to occur currently than in the 1960s and 1970s.

5. Most parents with adult children living at home are satisfied with the living arrangement and have mostly positive relationships with their adult children.

6. Neglect or abuse of frail elderly relatives is relatively common in the United States.

7. Loss of bladder control and cognitive impairment are common symptoms of normal aging.

8. The average annual income decreases after people reach age 55.

9. Retired people are more likely to suffer from sickness or depression than are people of the same age who still work.

10. Research conducted by Rowe and Lasswell on marriages lasting 50 or more years found that couples with larger families tended to have less happy marriages.

Short Answer

1. Give three definitions of *middle age* as presented in the text.

2. Describe the "two-step career" approach to life for women.

3. List three symptoms of menopause and three symptoms of "male menopause."

4. What is the "sandwich generation"?

5. Describe how aging is a biological phenomenon as well as psychological, social, and family phenomena.

Name _____   Chapter 13

PERSONAL INVOLVEMENT ASSESSMENT—
MY FAMILY LIFE CYCLE

Each one of us has some family of origin—whether it is the one into which we were born or adopted, or one of which we became part (such as a foster family). Undoubtedly, each of our families has faced many challenges, with individual members having to undergo various adjustments, including marital adjustments.

For this exercise, you will assess the adjustments and family relationships at different stages in your family's life cycle. You have a choice as to how to approach this assessment. Although you may devise an approach of your own choosing, three options follow.

Option 1. Obtain photographs of family members representing different generations—that is, your own children (if you have any), siblings, parents, grandparents, great-grandparents (if you have any), or any stepfamily members, as well as any other family members of importance to your development. If possible, include photographs of each of the family members involved at different ages. Prepare a short, modified family album that includes the photographs, brief descriptions of the family members, and designations of relationships to one another.

Option 2. Prepare a collage of illustrations cut out from magazines depicting individuals in various family roles, of different ages, and facing different types of marital and other types of family adjustment at the different stages in the family life cycle. Select illustrations that represent as much as possible members in your own family. Briefly describe the family members and relationships represented in the illustrations.

Option 3. Prepare a family tree of your immediate family up through your grandparents. Do what is asked in Options 1 and 2 but without pictures, illustrations, or photographs.

Marital/Family Adjustments of Family Members. As best as you are able and from your own perception, include descriptions of the marital and other family adjustments listed below that each family member—shown in the family album or represented in the collage or family tree—has experienced or is experiencing.

1. Beginning marriage adjustments:

2. Parenthood adjustments:

3. Midlife marital adjustments:

4. Postparental marital adjustments:

5. Late adulthood/elderly marital adjustments:

6. Widowhood adjustments:

Assessment. Review what you have written about marital/family adjustments throughout the family life cycle as you perceive them to exist in your family. How do these fit in with what is discussed in the chapter? Which, if any, particularly correspond; and which, if any, differ substantially? Discuss.

Name _____   Chapter 13

KNOWLEDGE IN ACTION—
TODAY'S GRANDPARENTS

The chapter discusses various myths about older people and how contemporary grandparents are different from those in the past or at least different from the stereotyped portrayals of grandparents in the past. Today's grandparents are more likely to live longer, be healthier longer, be more physically fit, and be freed from many of the past norms restricting their behavior.

Select one of the following exercises to complete:

Option 1: Interview. What are grandparents of today like? Conduct interviews with a "contemporary" grandmother and grandfather—either your own or someone else's. Develop questions ahead of time that pertain to points discussed in the chapter about today's grandparents: for example, they are younger in body than those of previous generations; they have stayed younger and healthier as a result of modern nutrition and improved medical care; they can be younger in mind and spirit by keeping up with modern trends and ideas through mass media, adult education, and travel. Summarize your findings.

Persons Interviewed.

Questions Asked.

Summary/Discussion.

(Attach another sheet of paper if needed.)

Option 2: Media Content Analysis. (1) Prepare a collage of photos or illustrations cut out of magazines, showing images of today's grandparents. Prepare a second collage showing images of grandparents in the past. Or (2) analyze roles of grandparents—both contemporary and from the past—that you have viewed on television or in film or have read about in books. Provide some examples and then summarize the differences.

Media Used.

Tally.

Discussion/Implications.

(Attach another sheet of paper if needed.)

ANSWER KEY

Key Terms

1. spacious nest
2. androgen
3. crisis-loss stage of grief
4. middle age
5. caught in the middle
6. new-life stage of grief
7. empty nest syndrome
8. sandwich generation
9. ageism
10. cluttered nest
11. transition stage of grief
12. Routinization
13. old age
14. Male menopause
15. longevis marriages
16. menopause
17. midlife crisis
18. Boomerang kids

Multiple Choice

1. b
2. c
3. c
4. a
5. c
6. a
7. a
8. b
9. c
10. a
11. c
12. b
13. c
14. d
15. b

True/False

1. F
2. F
3. T
4. F
5. T
6. T
7. F
8. T
9. F
10. T

Suggested Responses to Short Answer Questions

1. 1) "middlescence": middle years in which individuals mourn for lost opportunities and what their lives could have been like and yearn for taut young bodies and freedom from routines; 2) Erik Erikson's: a time for generativity or stagnation; 3) Bernice Neugarten's: the time when people begin to think of the time they have left, not how long they've already lived; 4) Evelyn Duvall's: the time between the last child's leaving home and retirement.

2. women returning to college or to work outside of the home once their children become more independent. Although these women are often at a disadvantage because they have been out of the workforce for a considerable period of time, they may find new energy and enthusiasm about starting off on a new "career" in their life.

3. Menopause: 1) shrinking of reproductive organs, 2) decrease in amount of fatty tissue in the breasts and other bodily parts, 3) thinning of vulva and shrinking of vagina, 4) decrease in amount of vaginal secretions, 5) possible irritability, hot flashes, headaches, depression. Male menopause: 1) declining of androgen, 2) diminishing of amount of ejaculate, 3) decrease in size and firmness of testicles, 4) less frequent and less rigid erections, 5) more time to reach orgasm.

4. Middle-aged parents who have responsibilities for children, adolescents, and/or boomerang kids at home as well as increasingly for their own aging parents.

5. *Biological:* decrease in good health and stamina as a result of different genetic heritages; *psychological:* how old one feels based on one's mental attitudes; *social:* social definitions of what one is like and should do based on one's age; *family:* ongoing interpersonal relationships with family members contribute to how one defines oneself as older.

CHAPTER 14

FAMILY STRESS AND COPING

CHAPTER OUTLINE

Cultural Perspective on Family Stress

The Curvilinear Nature of Stress
    Stress and Life Events
    Stress Pile-Up

Stressors for Families
    Common Types of Family Stressors
    Stressors Across the Family Life Cycle
    Common Life Events at All Stages of the Life Cycle
    Boundary Ambiguity and Family Stress

Family Stress Theory
    The ABC-X Model of Family Stress
    The Double ABC-X Family Stress Model
    A Roller Coaster Course of Adjustment
    Family System Changes in Response to a Major Stressor
    Families Who Manage Stress Successfully

Family Coping Strategies
    Theoretical Perspectives
    A Case Study
    A Cross-Cultural Analysis
    Social Support

The Biopsychological Approach and Family Problems
    Medical Care and the Family
    The Family's Influence on Health Behaviors

LEARNING OBJECTIVES

After reading Chapter 14, you should be able to:
- Understand that life is stressful and that it is important to balance the stress in one's life. Too much is harmful, but too little is also not good
- Discuss the biopsychosocial theory of stress
- Explain family stress theory
- Summarize the common stressors over the family life cycle
- Delineate the specific family stressors that affect at least 10 percent of families at each stage of the family life cycle
- Know why balanced families cope better with stress
- Explain *boundary ambiguity* and its connection to family stress

PRACTICE TESTS

Key Terms

1. _____ involves the effect of a family member's being physically and/or psychologically present or absent on the degree of stress associated with a situation.
2. A single event's becoming the "last straw" and turning into a crisis can occur as a result of _____.
3. The _____ delineates the impact stress can have on one's emotions and physiological well-being.
4. Reaction of the body to the demands of life constitutes _____.
5. A family _____ can occur when a turning point is reached as a result of some significant change for which customary ways of dealing are inadequate.
6. _____ involves a family's resolving a stressful situation without detrimental effects on any member.
7. A healthy kind of stress that is at a moderate to high level is referred to as _____.
8. A(n) _____ is a demand on the family that accompanies a stressor event.
9. External events, called _____, can cause emotional and/or physical reactions in individuals.
10. Unresolved residual effects of previous stressor events, or _____, may continue to be problematic for the family.
11. Feelings of discomfort, called _____, can be caused by too much stress in one's life.
12. A theoretical model of family crisis in which the focus is on a family's ability to adapt to a crisis is the _____.
13. A(n) _____ is one which has the potential to cause a crisis but which is considered neutral until its impact on the family is assessed.
14. The _____ is a theoretical model of family crisis that focuses on the family's ability to cope as a result of hardships resulting from a crisis and unresolved prior crises.
15. Redefining a stressful experience in a positive way as a coping strategy is _____.
16. A(n) _____, comprised of an interdependent group of family members, friends, and acquaintances, can be drawn upon as a resource in trying to cope with stress.
17. A therapeutic framework utilizing family systems theory and the biopsychosocial approach to deal with health problems in family members is _____.

Multiple Choice

1. Which statement about a paradoxical aspect of stress is true, according to Dahl?
   a. Distress occurs when one experiences too little stress.
   b. Stress that occurs beyond a moderate level, referred to as eustress, is usually unhealthy.
   c. The healthiest situation is for one to experience little or no stress.
   d. Too little stress is unhealthy and is often associated with boredom.
2. Results of a Gallup poll, as reported in the text, indicate that _____ were most likely to insist they didn't need help from anyone in changing their behavior.
   a. single women
   b. single men
   c. married women
   d. married men

3. Getting a divorce falls under which of the following different types of family stressors as identified by Boss?
   a. internal
   b. non-normative
   c. cumulative
   d. non-ambiguous

4. According to a 1985 Gallup poll, which of the following had the highest percentage for adults attempting to improve their health?
   a. reduced alcohol consumption
   b. lost weight
   c. became more careful about nutritional intake
   d. quit smoking

5. A family member's being an alcoholic falls under which of the following types of family stressors as identified by Boss?
   a. chronic
   b. cumulative
   c. volitional
   d. non-normative

6. Which type of stress and strain was indicated by young couples without children in a study by Olson and colleagues of seven family life stages?
   a. marital strains
   b. family transitions
   c. work-family strains
   d. losses

7. Olson et al. found that _____ were an area of stress and strain for couples in the childbearing stage.
   a. marital strains
   b. family transitions
   c. work-family strains
   d. losses

8. In Olson et al.'s study of stress and strain during family life stages, _____ was (were) found to be an area of concern for families with school-age children.
   a. pregnancy
   b. financial strains
   c. family transitions
   d. illnesses

9. Hill's "roller coaster course of adjustment" includes all of the following EXCEPT:
   a. a period of disorganization
   b. a sharp drop in coping ability
   c. an angle of recovery
   d. a new level of organization

10. Stress pile-up would most likely be applicable to the _____ of family crisis.
    a. ABC-X model
    b. Double ABC-X model
    c. roller coaster course model
    d. biopsychosocial model

11. Which of the following family life events was found to be more of concern than the others to most families in Olson and colleagues' study?
    a. sexual difficulties between husband and wife
    b. emotional difficulties in family life
    c. illness and death in the family
    d. money for the basics of family living

12. According to Boss, a family's coping resources are derived from all of the following aspects of life EXCEPT:
    a. psychological
    b. political
    c. sociological
    d. economic

13. Geiss and O'Leary's study with 250 therapists found that therapists ranked problems relating to _____ as the most destructive to a relationship.
    a. role conflict
    b. sex
    c. extramarital affairs
    d. communication

14. Which theory pertaining to stress deals with the cumulative effects of stress on families?
    a. biopsychosocial
    b. ABC-X Family Crisis Model
    c. Double ABC-X Family Stress Model
    d. boundary ambiguity

15. At which level of boundary ambiguity does Boss maintain that family stress is easiest to manage?
    a. high
    b. moderate-to-high
    c. low-to-moderate
    d. low

True/False

1. It does not matter whether stress is positive or negative in demand; both create the same physiological response.
2. Happiness is dependent upon being able to avoid stress.
3. Life events that create stress can be positive occurrences.
4. Recovery from a crisis, such as the birth of a stillborn baby, commonly takes longer for women than for men.
5. According to Olson and colleagues in their study of family life events, stress decreases dramatically among older couples whose children have left home.
6. According to Geiss and O'Leary, therapists report that extramarital affairs rank among the five most damaging problems.
7. Geiss and O'Leary report that therapists find alcoholism the most difficult marital problem to resolve.
8. Passive appraisal is defined as individual reflection on the details of a crisis that precedes positive decision making.
9. According to the authors, nearly 60 percent of U.S. families are plagued by alcohol-related problems.
10. Holmes and Rahe found a correlation between experiencing stress and developing health changes.

Short Answers

1. Explain what is meant by a curvilinear relationship between stress and functioning.

2. What is the difference between the ABC-X Family Crisis Model and the Double ABC-X Family Stress Model?

3. Identify the three stages of family adjustment to a crisis, as described by Hill. Provide an example for each using one type of family crisis.

4. Which types of families—balanced or unbalanced on the Circumplex Model—did Olson and his colleagues find cope better with stress, and why?

5. Give an example of both low and high levels of boundary ambiguity.

Name _____   Chapter 14

PERSONAL INVOLVEMENT ASSESSMENT—
STRESS SCALE

Chapter 14 includes a discussion of a scale developed by Holmes and Rahe (1967) having to do with life events requiring some change of behavior or readjustment. The Holmes and Rahe Social Readjustment Rating Scale, or Stress Scale, includes stressors having to do with occupational, marriage, and family issues. Holmes and Rahe found that individuals' health can be affected by their life changes, even so much as to bring about ulcers, cancer, depression, a heart attack, or the onset of alcoholism. These can occur even with positive life changes as a result of increased stress in one's life.

Assessment. Following each item (event) listed below, indicate the number of points out of 100 (100 being highest level of stress, 0 being lowest) that you believe would represent the level of stress you would feel (or have felt) from this event. For example, if you believe getting fired from your job would result in a moderate level of stress, write in 50; if you believe it would result in a rather high level of stress, but not overwhelming, write in 75 or 80.

Event	Points
1. Death of spouse	____
2. Divorce	____
3. Marital separation	____
4. Jail term	____
5. Death of close family member	____
6. Personal injury or loss	____
7. Marriage	____
8. Fired at work/lost job	____
9. Marital reconciliation	____
10. Retirement	____
11. Change in health of family member	____
12. Pregnancy	____
13. Sex difficulties	____
14. Gain of new family member	____
Total	____

Now, compare your points to those found from a sample of people as indicated in Table 16.1 in the text.

Reprinted by permission of the publisher from "The Social Readjustment Rating Scale" by T. H. Holmes and R. H. Rahe, Journal of Psychosomatic Research, 11, p. 213. Copyright © 1967 by Elsevier Science Inc.

Discuss how you compare with the averages of those sampled.

As indicated in the text, Holmes and Rahe found that those scoring total points within certain ranges had experienced a serious negative health change in the two years following the life event, for example:

0 to 150 points: more than 30 percent

151 to 300 points: about 50 percent

more than 300 points: almost 90 percent

Discuss your reactions to these figures. What could you do to minimize potential effects on your health?

Name _____   Chapter 14

KNOWLEDGE IN ACTION—
HOW MY FAMILY DEALS WITH STRESS

Chapter 14 presents several models, approaches, and strategies used by families in responding to and coping with stress. Identify a major stressor in your family, and describe how your family has dealt or is dealing with it. Identify which model, approach, or strategy described in the chapter best fits your family's situation, and discuss why this one is more applicable than the others.

Stressor:

How my family has dealt with this stressor:

Applicable model, approach, or strategy that fits my family situation.

Why this is more applicable than others.

ANSWER KEY

Key Terms

1. Boundary ambiguity
2. stress pile-up
3. biopsychosocial approach
4. stress
5. crisis
6. Family coping
7. eustress
8. family hardship
9. stressors
10. prior strains
11. distress
12. ABC-X Family Crisis Model
13. stressful life event
14. Double ABC-X Family Stress Model
15. reframing
16. social support network
17. medical family therapy

Multiple Choice

1. d
2. b
3. b
4. c
5. a
6. c
7. c
8. b
9. b
10. b
11. d
12. b
13. d
14. c
15. d

True/False

1. T
2. F
3. T
4. F
5. T
6. F
7. T
8. F
9. F
10. T

Suggested Responses to Short Answer Questions

1. Moderate levels of stress are usually positive, but either too little or too much stress can be problematic for individual and family functioning.

2. The first focuses on a single event giving rise to a family crisis, which can be handled positively or negatively depending on how the family tends to define and handle crises. The second focuses on how families handle the cumulative effects of stress rather than on a single event.

3. 1) A period of disorganization, 2) an angle of recovery, and 3) a new level of organization.

4. Balanced families cope better because they utilize better communication patterns and have a larger behavioral repertoire, including more personal and relationship resources and problem-solving skills.

5. *Low*: death of family member; *High*: alcoholic family member, kidnapped child.

CHAPTER 15

FAMILY PROBLEMS, DOMESTIC VIOLENCE, AND ALCOHOL ABUSE

CHAPTER OUTLINE

Family Problems and Family Systems Theory
    The Family and Mental Illness
    The Family and Alcohol Abuse

Physical Abuse and Neglect of Children
    Incidence
    The Impact on Children
    Transcending Abuse
    Families at Risk
    Treatment and Prevention

Sexual Abuse of Children
    Dynamics of Incestuous Families
    Effects of Sexual Abuse and Incest
    Treatment and Prevention

Spouse Abuse
    Incidence
    Factors Contributing to Spouse Abuse
    Patterns of Spouse Abuse
    Treatment and Prevention

Sibling and Child-to-Parent Abuse
    Sibling Abuse
    Child-to-Parent Abuse

Alcohol Problems in Families
    Alcohol As a "Cause" of Family Violence
    The Family's Reaction to Alcohol Abuse
    Treatment and Prevention of Alcoholism
    Acknowledging the Dangers of Legal Drugs

LEARNING OBJECTIVES

After reading Chapter 15, you should be able to:

- List the different forms of child maltreatment, discussing how prevalent they are and why they occur in all social classes and at all income levels
- Explain the two extreme behavioral adaptations children can have to abuse and how the cycle of violence can be broken
- Explain why child abuse, especially sexual abuse of children, has seemingly increased dramatically in recent years
- Discuss why domestic violence is the single greatest cause of injury to women and why most cases are not reported
- Identify alternatives available to women victims of domestic violence
- Understand the prevalence of alcohol abuse in our society and how it affects the lives of the majority of people in this country
- Summarize the ways in which families commonly react to and cope with alcohol abuse
- Realize that legal drugs like alcohol and nicotine cause more deaths in the United States than do illegal drugs, which are commonly associated with family and individual problems

PRACTICE TESTS

Key Terms

1. _____, or re-experiencing of the event through mental flashbacks, is frequently found among victims of incest.
2. Self-help groups for families of alcoholics are part of _____.
3. _____ occurs more frequently than many believe, with about 10 percent of parents experiencing this form of family violence.
4. _____ explains that battered women frequently stay with their victimizers because they learned in childhood to be submissive and passive.
5. _____ involves the sexual exploitation of a child under 18 by a relative.
6. A family member who enables another family member to continue abusing alcohol is a(n) _____.
7. Delusions are frequent in the mental disorder of _____.
8. _____ is believed to occur among children in a majority of homes, mainly through physical aggression.
9. A functional disability resulting from consumption of alcohol is referred to as _____.
10. _____ offers support for young people with alcoholic parents.
11. An individual, usually a family member, whose actions reinforce an alcoholic's continued dependency on alcohol is referred to as a co-dependent, or _____.
12. Perpetrators of incest in the _____ are rarely found guilty.
13. Meetings of _____ self-help groups are held around the country to offer support and advice for troubled individuals.
14. The theory of _____, having to do with the venting of aggression verbally serving as a substitute for physical aggression, has not been substantiated.
15. The _____ tends to have multiple and long-lasting problems that contribute to the occurrence of incest within the family.
16. According to family systems theory, a _____ is likely to have grown up in a home where family violence took place.
17. _____ argues that what one family member does affects the entire family and that therapy should focus on helping the entire family function better, not just on helping one troubled member of the family.
18. _____ is an umbrella term including physical abuse, abandonment, neglect, emotional abuse, and sexual abuse of anyone younger than 18.
19. Sexual activity between members of the same family is called _____.
20. _____ is the fourth leading cause of death in the United States.
21. _____ is a mental disorder characterized by panic attacks.
22. _____ is more common among men than among women but is increasing among women.

Multiple Choice

1. Panic attacks are characteristic of:
   a. schizophrenia
   b. anxiety-neurotic illness
   c. alcoholism
   d. hallucinations

2. Which theoretical approach provides strong support for family systems theory, holding that the family, not just the troubled member, is not functioning well?
   a. family dynamics
   b. child development model
   c. Circumplex Model
   d. learned helplessness model

3. Zigler and his colleagues have estimated that about _____ of individuals who are physically or sexually abused or neglected as children will subject their own children to similar maltreatment.
   a. one-tenth
   b. one-fourth to one-third
   c. one-third to one-half
   d. two-thirds

4. The most commonly reported type of child maltreatment is:
   a. neglect
   b. physical abuse
   c. emotional abuse
   d. sexual abuse

5. The person most commonly responsible for the physical abuse of children is the child's:
   a. parent
   b. sibling
   c. peer
   d. child-care provider/babysitter

6. The effects of incest on children are thought to be similar to those of:
   a. post-traumatic stress disorder
   b. learned helplessness syndrome
   c. anxiety-neurotic illness
   d. schizophrenia

7. Which of Courtois' dynamics of understanding incestuous families has to do with the backgrounds of the family members?
   a. psychodynamic
   b. sociological
   c. family system
   d. feminist

8. Abusers in a _____ family are more likely to be punished for incest than are abusers in a _____ family—and their punishment is likely to be more severe.
   a. normal-appearing; chaotic
   b. normal-appearing; enmeshed
   c. chaotic; normal-appearing
   d. chaotic; enmeshed

9. Which statement best reflects the approach taken today by courts in dealing with father-daughter incest?
   a. Place the daughter in another home, e.g., a foster home or relative's home.
   b. Remove the father from the home.
   c. Develop an approach appropriate for the family's circumstances, e.g., help the family come to terms with the trauma.
   d. Incarcerate the father.

10. According to the National Center for Health Statistics, alcoholism has been present in the families of _____ adult Americans.
    a. one in ten
    b. four in ten
    c. one in four
    d. one in two

11. Which theoretical perspective is most likely to attribute a tendency toward domestic violence to an abuser's having learned to be a victimizer by having grown up in a violent home?
    a. family systems
    b. psychodynamic
    c. feminist
    d. behaviorist

12. Which perspective on likelihood of spouse abuse is reflected by feelings of inadequacy on the part of the abusive spouse?
    a. family systems theory
    b. learned helplessness theory
    c. low self-esteem
    d. social isolation

13. Which has NOT been found to be true regarding domestic violence?
    a. Police departments are now more likely to make arrests in domestic violence cases than in the past.
    b. The more that verbal aggressiveness takes place in a relationship, the greater the likelihood that physical aggressiveness will take place.
    c. Economic stress increases the likelihood of domestic violence.
    d. A man is more likely to kill his partner while she is still living with him than after she has left him.

14. Those theorists holding a _____ perspective believe that a patriarchal family system contributes to domestic violence because it socializes males to believe that aggression is an acceptable and normal response to stress and anger.
    a. family systems
    b. psychodynamic
    c. feminist
    d. behaviorist

15. According to Jackson, which stage in the process of families' attempting to live with an alcohol-abusing member is precipitated by the abuser's problematic behavior, such as mismanaging family funds or becoming violent toward another family member?
    a. Stage 2: The family tries to eliminate the problem.
    b. Stage 3: The family becomes disorganized.
    c. Stage 4: The family makes a first attempt at reorganization.
    d. Stage 5: The family attempts to escape the problem.

True/False

1. Clarke in his study of four groups of families found that unbalanced family types are less functional than balanced family types.
2. Researchers have been unable to find a relationship between a family's likeliness to be an unbalanced family and the family's having an alcohol-dependent member.
3. Child abuse and neglect are more likely to occur in low-income families.
4. Mothers are slightly less likely than fathers to engage in violent or severely violent behavior with their children.
5. Individuals who were abused as children are highly likely to become child abusers as adults.
6. At least 30,000 nonsmoking Americans die each year from breathing "secondhand" smoke.
7. Children in single-parent families are more likely to be abused than those living with two parents.
8. As a result of increased public awareness and intervention and prevention programs, reportings of child sexual abuse are declining.
9. The rate of spouse abuse has declined slightly in recent years.
10. Legal drugs cause more deaths each year than do illegal ones.

Short Answer

1. What are likely effects of child abuse on children?

2. Identify the three strategies suggested by Goldstein, Keller, and Erne for treating the family problem of child maltreatment.

3. Explain how incest can be viewed as an abuse of power and authority.

4. Identify the differences between the chaotic family and the normal-appearing family in relation to incest.

5. Identify the three phases of the cyclical pattern to spouse abuse.

Name _____   Chapter 15

PERSONAL INVOLVEMENT ASSESSMENT—
CHILD SEXUAL ABUSE

One form of child abuse is child sexual abuse. Most experts in the field seem to agree that about one in three or four girls will be sexually abused in some form by the time she reaches adulthood, and about one in six boys. Many believe that the rate is higher among boys, but that because of fears of being labeled as homosexual or weak, they are less likely to disclose the abuse than are girls. An estimated 90 percent of the offenders are known to the child.

While the legal definition varies by state, the National Center on Child Abuse and Neglect defines child sexual abuse as

> contacts or interaction between a child and an adult when the child is being used for the sexual stimulation of the perpetrator or another person. Sexual abuse may also be committed by a person under the age of 18 when that person is either significantly older than the victim or when the perpetrator is in a position of power or control over the victim.[1]

Assessment. What do you know about child sexual abuse? Take the following quiz on child sexual abuse, then compare your responses to the correct answers. Note the areas that appear to be well known and those that are less known. Discuss your findings.

Quiz. Answer True or False.[2]

_____ 1. Sexual molestation of children is usually a single, violent incident.

_____ 2. Sexual molestation of children usually begins in adolescence.

_____ 3. Sexual contact with a child is illegal even if the child consents.

_____ 4. Child sexual abuse doesn't occur unless an adult forces a child to have intercourse.

_____ 5. A large majority of child victims are molested by a family member or another person known to the child.

_____ 6. Nonviolent sexual abuse or coercion is less traumatic than aggressive or violent abuse.

_____ 7. A key component in defining child sexual abuse is the unequal power relationship between offender and child.

_____ 8. Many offenders were molested as children.

_____ 9. Boys who have been victimized tend to become homosexual adults.

_____ 10. Most sex offenders are heterosexual males.

_____ 11. Children can be psychologically harmed by the reaction of significant adults upon disclosure.

_____ 12. Children rarely make up stories about engaging in sexual activities with adults.

_____ 13. Direct disclosure of sexual abuse is more likely than indirect or disguised disclosure.

_____ 14. Venereal disease in children is a primary cause of suspicion of child sexual abuse.

_____ 15. Mandated reporters (professionals, such as physicians, required by state law to report suspected abuse) are expected to investigate suspected child sexual abuse.

---

[1] U.S. Department of Health, Education, and Welfare, *Child Sexual Abuse: Incest, Assault, and Sexual Exploration,* Publication No. 79-30166, 2.
[2] Committee for Children, Seattle, Washington.

_____ 16. A report should be regarded as a request for an investigation into a suspected incident of abuse.

_____ 17. The majority of cases of child sexual abuse are reported.

_____ 18. The majority of reported cases of child sexual abuse go to court.

_____ 19. Most states have mandatory prison sentences for offenders convicted of abuse.

_____ 20. Child sexual abuse happens at about the same rate in all kinds of neighborhoods and in all parts of the country.

Answers:

1. F	6. F	11. T	16. T
2. F	7. T	12. T	17. F
3. T	8. T	13. F	18. F
4. F	9. F	14. T	19. F
5. T	10. T	15. F	20. T

Your Score (number correct): _____

What, if anything, surprised you about this information on child sexual abuse?

Name _____   Chapter 15

KNOWLEDGE IN ACTION—
ASSISTANCE TO FAMILIES

Chapter 15 discusses some of the treatment programs that aid families experiencing various family crises. Across the country, a consensus has been building among social and government agencies about general principles that best help guide policies and programs aimed at strengthening families. This consensus characterizes agencies as having a "support" role to help the health, growth, and development of families. The main participants are the family members themselves.

Project. Identify a social agency or government office in your community that provides programs that assist families in crisis. (The telephone book and reference librarians are both good resources.) Ask to interview a staff person or an administrator of the agency or office you select. Develop questions ahead of time about the underlying principles that guide policy and program development. Obtain published policy statements if available. Discuss your views on the program or service.

Name of Program.

Name of Sponsoring Agency or Government Office.

Findings.

Discussion.

184 CHAPTER 15

ANSWER KEY

Key Terms

1. post-traumatic stress disorder
2. Al-Anon
3. child-to-parent abuse
4. learned helplessness theory
5. Incestuous abuse
6. co-dependent
7. schizophrenia
8. sibling abuse
9. problem drinking
10. Alateen
11. enabler
12. normal-appearing family
13. Alcoholics Anonymous
14. catharsis conflict
15. chaotic family
16. victimizer
17. family systems theory
18. child maltreatment
19. incest
20. alcoholism
21. anxiety disorder
22. alcohol abuse

Multiple Choice

1. b
2. c
3. b
4. a
5. b
6. a
7. a
8. c
9. c
10. b
11. a
12. c
13. d
14. c
15. c

True/False

1. T
2. F
3. T
4. F
5. F
6. T
7. T
8. F
9. T
10. T

Suggested Responses to Short Answer Questions

1. Due to their having been abused, mistreated children are likely to respond negatively to their parent(s), which is likely to produce a negative response from the parent(s), and so on. They also are likely to do poorly in school and to be aggressive and untrusting, have poor self-images, and become involved in delinquency and crime.

2. 1) increasing the parent's self-esteem, 2) increasing the parent's knowledge of children and positive childrearing techniques, and 3) devising community support networks for families under stress.

3. A child cannot give informed consent to any form of sexual activity with an adult.

4. The chaotic family, the stereotypically incestuous family, has multiple problems existing for many generations, e.g., substance abuse and trouble with the law. Often it is low in socioeconomic status, education, and vocation. Members are more likely to be punished and to be punished more severely for incest than are members of normal-appearing families. The normal-appearing family appears functional, is socially and financially stable, and is well-integrated into the community. It tends to follow traditional family roles, but its members are emotionally needy, with children often the caretakers for the parents.

5. 1) A tension-building phase; 2) an explosion phase, in which the actual beating occurs; and 3) a loving or honeymoon phase, in which the battered spouse is rewarded for staying in the relationship.

CHAPTER 16

DIVORCE AND ADJUSTMENT

CHAPTER OUTLINE

Trends in Divorce
    Statistical Trends
    Historical Trends
    Legal Trends

Understanding Divorce
    Why Couples Divorce
    Unhappy Versus Happy Couples

Adjusting to Divorce
    Emotional Divorce
    Legal Divorce
    Economic Divorce
    Coparental Divorce
    Community Divorce
    Psychological Divorce
    How Long Does It Take to Adjust?

LEARNING OBJECTIVES

After reading Chapter 16, you should be able to:
- Understand the prevalence of divorce in today's society and why it is not an entirely bad alternative
- Explain how no-fault divorce laws institute the norm of equality between the sexes
- Discuss Paul Bohannan's conceptualization of the divorce process as an intense emotional journey
- Weigh the effects of marital discord and divorce on children
- Know that divorce is a part of many people's lives, but that there is life after divorce

PRACTICE TESTS

Key Terms

1. A major scenario for divorce is a _____, which is reflected in a relationship gone stale and one in which one (or both) of the partners has gradually lost feeling for the other.

2. The increase of women in poverty in this country, or the _____, is in part due to the increasing divorce rate and the severe reduction in women's income.

3. The financial legacy of divorce is the _____.

4. The _____, one of the six stations of divorce, concerns the misery of divorce, which is often reflected in anger and violence; emotional disrepair, depression, and loneliness; and even in increased disease and illness.

5. Under traditional divorce law, _____ was privately agreed to by both parties, with no challenges occurring in the courts.

6. _____, providing continued financial support for former spouses following divorce, is less likely to be awarded under no-fault divorce than under traditional divorce law.

7. As opposed to traditional divorce law, _____ eliminates fault, or guilt of one party, as the basis for dissolving a marriage.

8. Shifting from being part of a couple to an independent lifestyle and identity is the _____.

9. Establishing arrangements pertaining to custody and visitation rights for noncustodial parents makes up the _____.

10. That part of divorce concerned with the legal arena, property, and custody agreements is the _____.

11. The _____, under traditional divorce law, presumed that the custody of young children should be given to their mother, who would be better able to take care of them.

12. Legal blame for the end of a marriage, or _____, was assigned under traditional divorce law but not now under no-fault divorce law.

13. Changes in relationships with friends, neighbors, and relatives are involved in the _____.

14. _____, having an extramarital relationship with someone, has been one of the major reasons cited by divorced persons for the failure of their marriages.

Multiple Choice

1. About ____ percent of young couples who divorce are likely to remarry.
   a. 50
   b. 58
   c. 65
   d. 75

2. Which statement about divorce is NOT true?
   a. Divorce is higher among lower-income couples.
   b. Divorce is higher among blacks than whites.
   c. Divorce is more likely to occur among religiously mixed marriages.
   d. Divorce occurs more frequently among those who marry at an older age.

3. The average length of first marriages that end is divorce is about _____ years.
   a. two
   b. four
   c. seven
   d. nine
4. What was one benefit of traditional divorce law for those having a valid grievance that was eliminated with no-fault divorce?
   a. fair property settlements
   b. equitable child custody arrangements
   c. a bargaining advantage for women in negotiating property settlements and alimony
   d. ability to have a court hearing before the final decree of divorce
5. The average age at divorce is _____ for men and _____ for women.
   a. 28; 26
   b. 32; 30
   c. 35; 33
   d. 40; 38
6. During which time period did the divorce rate reach its highest peak?
   a. middle to late 1960s
   b. late 1970s and early 1980s
   c. middle to late 1980s
   d. early 1990s
7. The most difficult period of divorce for males and females is:
   a. before the decision to divorce
   b. after the decision, but before the final decree
   c. just after the divorce
   d. one year later
8. The authors estimate that _____ percent of the children of divorced parents live with their mothers.
   a. 75
   b. 80
   c. 85
   d. 90
9. When did the divorce rate level off?
   a. late 1970s
   b. early 1980s
   c. late 1980s
   d. early 1990s
10. Which reason for divorce is often thought by researchers to be a result rather than a cause of marital problems?
    a. extramarital sex
    b. emotional problems
    c. physical abuse
    d. alcoholism
11. A surprise finding from Fowers and Olson's study of over 5,000 married couples was the little difference between happy and unhappy couples in:
    a. the quality of their sexual relationship
    b. their skills at resolving conflict
    c. the length of their marriage
    d. the quality of their communication

12. According to Albrecht, the largest percentage of divorced people characterize their divorce experience as:
    a. traumatic, a nightmare
    b. stressful, but bearable
    c. unsettling, but easier than expected
    d. relatively painless

13. Which of Bohannan's stations of divorce can result in increased disease and illness?
    a. emotional
    b. economic
    c. community
    d. psychological

14. Which of Bohannan's stations of divorce frequently results in drastic downward mobility?
    a. emotional
    b. economic
    c. legal
    d. coparental

15. Which has NOT been a major finding of research on the effects of divorce on children?
    a. Divorce is a very difficult crisis in the lives of most children who experience it.
    b. Many children become angry at their parents and at themselves.
    c. Family discord has more of a negative effect on children than does the type of marriage structure.
    d. The effects of divorce on children are always more negative than the effects on them of being in a family with unhappy parents.

True/False

1. More women than men are likely to remarry following divorce.
2. The "tender years" doctrine currently serves as the guideline for determining custody of children.
3. No-fault divorce has resulted in increased rates of divorce.
4. According to Spanier and Thompson, extramarital sex is more a result of than the cause of marital problems.
5. Most divorced people feel good about their property settlement.
6. More divorced women than men experience economic hardship.
7. Most experts agree that children do better in an intact two-parent family regardless of its stability than in a one-parent family.
8. Divorce rates are higher among the poor and low-income couples than among the educated and better off.
9. Although the divorce rate in the United States is high, it is no higher than the average of all other Western industrialized nations.
10. No-fault divorce, as expected, has resulted in greater economic equity for men and women following divorce.

Short Answer

1. Cite three common explanations for the dramatic rise in divorces.

2. Name and briefly describe the four major elements of traditional divorce law that were changed by the no-fault system of divorce.

3. Describe how each of the four elements of traditional divorce law has been changed under no-fault divorce law.

4. Cite three findings of Dixon and Weitzman's evaluation of the no-fault system.

5. List and define three of Bohannan's six stations of divorce.

Name _____   Chapter 16

PERSONAL INVOLVEMENT ASSESSMENT—
THE DIVORCE EXPERIENCE

Stan Albrecht wrote in 1980 of the "best" and "worst" periods of divorce according to women and men who had participated in research he conducted. The results are found in Table 16.2 in the text and are broken down by female, male, and combined sample. Albrecht also indicated for whom—the husband or wife—the situation was better or worse.

Project. Place an X in front of the item you believe fits best in terms of how you think you *would* likely react if you were to get a divorce or how you *did* react if you have gone through a divorce.

1. <u>Characterization of divorce experience</u>:

    ____ Traumatic, a nightmare

    ____ Stressful, but bearable

    ____ Unsettling, but easier than expected

    ____ Relatively painless

2. <u>Most difficult period</u>:

    ____ Before decision to divorce

    ____ After decision, but before final decree

    ____ Just after the divorce

    ____ Now

3. <u>Best time for self and children</u>:

    ____ Before decision to divorce

    ____ After decision, but before final decree

    ____ Just after the divorce

    ____ Now

4. <u>Feeling about property settlement</u>:

    ____ Good or very good

    ____ Frustrated, unhappy

    ____ Just glad to get out

5. <u>Postdivorce income</u>:

    ____ Much lower

    ____ Somewhat lower

    ____ About the same

    ____ Somewhat higher

    ____ Much higher

DIVORCE AND ADJUSTMENT   193

6. <u>Change in contact with relatives</u>:

___ More contact

___ No change

___ Less contact

Now, contrast your responses to the percentages listed in Table 16.2 in the text. Briefly indicate how yours compare with those from the study.

1. <u>Characterization of divorce experience</u>:

2. <u>Most difficult period</u>:

3. <u>Best time for self and children</u>:

4. <u>Feeling about property settlement</u>:

5. <u>Postdivorce income</u>:

6. <u>Change in contact with relatives</u>:

Name _____   Chapter 16

KNOWLEDGE IN ACTION—
CHILD VISITATION

One of the most difficult aspects of divorce is the effect on the children. Part of the difficulty, of course, is that children usually live with one of the parents and visit the other. Much has been written about the negative consequences for children of conflict involving custodial situations. Nevertheless, there can be benefits for children in terms of learning responsibility by helping their single parents.

Select one of the following exercises to complete:

Option 1: Divorce/Child-Custody Court. Visit a local courtroom in which a dissolution (divorce) child-custody case is being heard. If possible, observe throughout the hearing. Attempt to learn as much as you can about the parents' perspectives on the divorce and their motivations for wanting custody of their child(ren). Observe witnesses and the children themselves.

Date and Location of Observation.

Background of Case.

Observations.

Discussion.

(Attach another sheet of paper if needed.)

Option 2: Interview. How do children feel about divorce of their parents and visitation with one parent? Conduct an interview with a child or children you know whose parents are divorced, or interview a parent who has been divorced. Develop questions ahead of time that pertain to their feelings about the divorce, their present arrangements, and what they think of visitations with the parent not residing with them (or with their children not residing with them).

Child(ren) Interviewed.

Date/Location.

Questions Asked.

Results.

Implications.

(Attach another sheet of paper if needed.)

ANSWER KEY

Key Terms

1. devitalized (burned-out) marriage
2. feminization of poverty
3. economic divorce
4. emotional divorce
5. uncontested divorce
6. Alimony
7. no-fault divorce
8. psychological divorce
9. coparental divorce
10. legal divorce
11. tender years doctrine
12. fault
13. community divorce
14. Infidelity

Multiple Choice

1. d
2. d
3. c
4. c
5. c
6. b
7. a
8. b
9. c
10. a
11. c
12. b
13. a
14. b
15. d

True/False

1. F
2. F
3. F
4. T
5. T
6. T
7. F
8. T
9. F
10. F

Suggested Responses to Short Answer Questions

1. Changes in divorce laws; women's liberation; social factors, including economic conditions, level of education of women, and attitudes toward divorce; free choice in marital selection; relative economic independence of women; decrease in religious significance of marriage bond.

2. 1) Sex-based divisions of role responsibilities: husband the provider, continued support after divorce if wife had remained virtuous, wife the preferred custodial parent; 2) grounds for divorce: legal blame, or fault, assigned to one party in order for marriage to end, or divorce was uncontested, with both parties agreeing to one of them being blamed; 3) adversarial proceedings: lawyers representing the parties battled in order for one party to win and the other to be judged guilty; 4) linkage of the financial settlement to determination of fault: financial consequences, in the form of alimony and/or property awards, linked to a finding of guilty or innocent.

3. 1) Elimination of fault-based grounds for divorce: no more having to prove guilt of one party—replaced by "irreconcilable differences"; 2) elimination of the adversarial process: accurate and responsible communication facilitates amicable divorce and joint custody of children; 3) basing of financial decisions on equity, equality, and economic need rather than on fault or sex-based role assignments: support payments based on economic need with encouragement for divorced women to be self-supporting; this has been shown to have had a negative consequence on many women and their children and a positive consequence for ex-husbands; 4) redefinition of the traditional duties of husbands and wives and establishment of equality between the sexes as a norm: both spouses are presumed to be equal partners (the husband is not assumed to be the head of the family); both are treated the same with regard to obligations for support and care of their children.

4. The divorce rate has not increased as a result, the mandatory counseling feature has not brought about many reconciliations, the hypocrisy of the old system has been eliminated, the number of divorce hearings has declined, property settlements and support appear to be fairer, but the bargaining advantage of women, in particular, in negotiating property settlements and alimony has been eliminated.

5. 1) The emotional divorce: the feelings associated with ending a marriage, often expressed in anger and violence, depression, loneliness; 2) the legal divorce: conflict associated with the legal process and having to work out arrangements through others, e.g., attorneys; 3) the economic divorce: problems associated both with property settlements and custody arrangements and with the economic consequences of the divorce, e.g., less money, many women having to enter or return to the job market; 4) the co-parental divorce: dealing with custody, single-parent homes, visitation rights; 5) the community divorce: changes in friendship, kinship, and community relations; 6) the psychological divorce: adjusting to being without the former spouse, being single, starting to date, etc.

CHAPTER 17

SINGLE-PARENT FAMILIES AND STEPFAMILIES

CHAPTER OUTLINE

The Changing Picture of the Family
    The Increase in Single-Parent Families
    Family Terminology
    Growing Family Complexity
    Differences Between Nuclear Families and Stepfamilies

Single-Parent Families
    Mothers with Custody
    Fathers with Custody
    Split Custody
    Joint Custody
    Coping Successfully as a Single Parent

Stepfamilies
    Stages in the Formation of a Stepfamily
    Guidelines for Stepfamilies
    Strengths of Stepfamilies

LEARNING OBJECTIVES

After reading Chapter 17, you should be able to:
- List and discuss the four different types of divorced single-parent families, explaining why different families need different approaches to living after a divorce
- Summarize good advice for new single parents
- List some of the challenges stepparents face, as well as some reasons why living in a stepfamily can be a very rewarding experience
- Understand that strengths found in single-parent families and in stepfamilies are similar to those seen in other types of families

PRACTICE TESTS

Key Terms

1. The melding together of two families and children as a result of remarriage, a(n) _____ might more appropriately be referred to as a reconstituted family.

2. A(n) _____ includes children of both new spouses in a remarriage.

3. _____ can occur when new stepfamily members create a false sense of togetherness rather than genuine togetherness based on open, honest, straightforward communication patterns.

4. A program developed by Visher and Visher to help stepfamilies survive is the _____.

5. _____ involves both parents having equal importance in providing homes for their children.

6. A family in which there are children unrelated biologically or through adoption to a new spouse of the parent is a(n) _____.

7. _____ can include both the marrying again of a former spouse and marrying a new partner following divorce or the death of the first partner.

8. A family composed of children biologically related to one parent and residing with a stepparent is a _____.

9. A(n) _____ is one related to children by having married the children's mother or father.

10. The parent having _____ of the children following divorce has the responsibility for the primary home for the children.

11. A premarital inventory developed by Olson and his colleagues and used helping couples prepare for a marriage that will result in a stepfamily is _____.

12. The establishment of two households following divorce, the mother's and the father's, results in a _____ family as long as both former spouses stay involved with their children.

13. One parent's having sole custody of one or more of the children and the other parent's having sole custody of one or more of the children after divorce is _____.

Multiple Choice

1. As of 1994, the proportion of single-parent families was _____ percent.
    a. 11
    b. 18
    c. 24
    d. 31

2. _____ have the largest percentage of single parents.
    a. Caucasians
    b. African Americans
    c. Mexican Americans
    d. Asian Americans

3. Schultz, Schultz, and Olson found the following in their study of stepfamilies:
    a. Simple stepfamilies have more strengths than complex stepfamilies.
    b. Complex stepfamilies have more strengths than simple stepfamilies.
    c. No difference was found in strengths between simple and complex stepfamilies.
    d. Each type of stepfamilies has strength over the other.

4. The term *binuclear family* can be used in place of the term:
   a. stepfamily
   b. single-parent family
   c. blended family
   d. reconstituted family

5. Which term do some professionals prefer for the new family formed when two adults with children marry?
   a. binuclear family
   b. joint family
   c. reorganizing family
   d. reconstituted family

6. The percentage of single-parent families headed by fathers had increased to ____ percent as of 1994.
   a. 7
   b. 10
   c. 16
   d. 22

7. _____ is the least common of the parenting options after divorce.
   a. Mothers with sole custody
   b. Fathers with sole custody
   c. Split-custody families
   d. Joint-custody families

8. Which single-parent group is the LEAST common?
   a. widows
   b. divorced fathers
   c. never-married fathers
   d. widowers

9. What is the average length of time before people remarry following divorce?
   a. one to two years
   b. two to three years
   c. three to four years
   d. four to five years

10. According to McGoldrick and Carter, which stage in the process of forming a new family through remarriage involves restructuring family boundaries?
    a. entering a new relationship
    b. planning the new marriage and family
    c. remarriage and reconstitution of the family
    d. achieving an "emotional divorce" from the former spouses

11. What is the main objection of Visher and Visher to the term *blended family*?
    a. The label assumes unrealistic expectations that the new family will easily become a harmonious family.
    b. The term assumes a homogeneous unit without previous history of being together.
    c. The term suffers from many stereotypes.
    d. The term does not take into consideration continuing problems with the former spouse(s).

12. During which stage in the process of forming a new family through remarriage is it important that pseudomutuality be avoided?
    a. entering a new relationship
    b. planning the new marriage and family
    c. remarriage and reconstitution of the family
    d. achieving an "emotional divorce" from the former spouses

13. What appears to be the major reason for single-parent families to have gotten a "bad press" from researchers?
    a. They have so many problems.
    b. They are viewed as "broken families."
    c. Researchers have often obtained their samples from clinical populations, thus focusing on dysfunctional aspects of some families.
    d. Single-parent family heads report that they are not happy.

14. An estimated _____ percent of younger men and women who divorce will likely remarry.
    a. 45
    b. 55
    c. 65
    d. 75

15. About _____ of noncustodial parents do not make full child-support payments.
    a. one-fifth
    b. one-fourth
    c. one-third
    d. one-half

True/False

1. As used in the text, the term *remarriage* refers to marrying the same person for a second time.
2. A stepfamily is a nuclear family.
3. Pink and Wampler's study of stepfamilies and first-marriage families using the Family Circumplex Model found that family cohesion and flexibility were indicated as being higher in first-marriage families than in stepfamilies.
4. DeFrain and Eirick, in their study comparing divorced single fathers and divorced single mothers, found no significant statistical differences between the two groups in adjustments to divorce.
5. Parents who agree to joint custody are more likely to come out of a burned-out marriage than one in which there was dislike or hatred for the former spouse.
6. Single-parent families generally have more problems than two-parent families.
7. According to Schultz, Schultz, and Olson, simple stepfamilies and complex stepfamilies show no significant differences in strengths.
8. Parents who have joint-custody arrangements report less stress than single-custody parents do.
9. Second marriages ending in divorce usually do so sooner than do first marriages.
10. The majority of people will divorce and remarry rather than marry only one time.

Short Answer

1. List and define three of the four types of relationship behaviors between ex-spouses described by Ahrons and Rodgers.

2. Name the four categories of divorced single-parent families as identified by DeFrain, Fricke, and Elmen.

3. Name the three steps involved in forming a new family through remarriage, as identified by McGoldrick and Carter, and briefly discuss the requisite feature(s) of each.

4. Discuss five differences between nuclear families and stepfamilies.

5. Identify three major problems for mothers and/or fathers with sole custody.

Name _____   Chapter 17

PERSONAL INVOLVEMENT ASSESSMENT—
"GHOSTS AND TRIANGLES"

Each remarriage involves both "ghosts" and "triangles." The ghosts are the comparisons made between the present spouse and the former spouse, the remembrances of both the negative and the positive aspects of former relationships. The triangles are the present involvements of each spouse as a result of previous marriages—the present relationships with former spouses, children from the former marriage(s), and even former in-laws. Competing claims tend to develop between various sets of children and from the former spouse(s) and the present spouse. Broderick specifies the following sets of triangular relationships, all of which a woman might have to deal with (or a man, with a former and current wife):

- Triangle 1: Herself, her former husband, and her present husband. As long as husband 1 is the father of her children, this triangle cannot be avoided.
- Triangle 2: Herself, her former husband, and the children of that marriage.
- Triangle 3: Herself, her current husband, and his former wife.
- Triangle 4: Herself, her current husband, and his children by his former marriage.
- Triangle 5: Herself, her former husband, and his new wife.
- Triangle 6: Herself, her children by her former marriage, and her current husband's children by his former marriage.
- Triangle 7: Herself, her children by her former marriage, and the children by her current husband.
- Triangle 8: Herself, her current husband's children by his former marriage, and their children together in this marriage.
- Triangle 9: Herself, her children by her former marriage, and her former husband's children in his current marriage.
- Triangle 10: Herself, her former husband, and her children by her current marriage.
- Triangle 11: Herself, her former husband, and the children of her new husband's former marriage.
- Triangle 12: Herself, the children of her current husband's former marriage, and the mother of those children (his former wife).

Source for this section is Carlfred B. Broderick, *Marriage and the Family*, 3rd ed. (Englewood Cliffs,: N.J. Prentice-Hall, 1988), 376. © 1988 Prentice-Hall. Reprinted by permission of the publisher.

Assessment. After reading over the list of triangular relationships, answer the following questions:

1. Have you or anyone you know well been involved in a remarriage, blended, or stepfamily situation? If so, briefly describe.

2. Which triangles does it fit?

3. What have been the positive and negative aspects of the situation?

4. Now, write a very brief synopsis of how you might explain the relationships involved to a child (real or hypothetical). Indicate the child's age, gender, and other relevant information.

(Attach an additional sheet of paper if needed.)

Name _____   Chapter 17

KNOWLEDGE IN ACTION—
THE STATIONS OF REMARRIAGE

As was brought out in the text, remarriage may work out better for many people because they're more experienced and usually more mature; nevertheless, it still can pose problems. These problems often involve children from former marriages. A related problem can be the lack of societal guidelines for remarried couples.

Ann Goetting's "six stations of remarriage" are the developmental tasks people go through when adjusting to remarriage. (Note the closeness of them to the six stations of *divorce* developed by Bohannan (1970) as described in Chapter 16.) They are as follow:

1. **Emotional Remarriage:** The first step is the process in which a divorced individual gradually reestablishes attraction, commitment, and trust in a bond with someone other than her or his former partner. This period can be marked by fear of the involvement leading to loss and rejection.

2. **Psychic Remarriage:** This stage is marked by the transition from individual to couple in the individual's conjugal identity; it is also the stage when others begin to view the two people as part of a partnership. Generally, this transition represents less change and a smoother transition for men than for women, and for women in traditional roles than for women in nontraditional roles.

3. **Community Remarriage:** Friendships are lost and friendships are gained in this stage, as couples typically become more involved with married-couple friends and less with unmarried friends. This stage can be very stressful because of the loss of valued friendship bonds.

4. **Parental Remarriage:** This stage, frequently the most difficult, is necessary when children from former marriages are involved. Becoming a stepparent can be very difficult, largely due to the lack of a clear role definition in our society and the lack of establishment of parental role expectations between the two partners (these probably would have been established if the partners had gone through a pregnancy together).

5. **Economic Remarriage:** This stage involves the establishment of the new marital household as an economic unit of productivity and consumption. Many researchers in the field believe that problems of finances are second only to problems of children in a remarriage. Although the standard of living usually increases with remarriage, there can be great stress and instability when stepchildren are involved, largely because of lack of consistency in child-support payments. Another problem is resource distribution—how the money should be spent.

6. **Legal Remarriage:** Many legal considerations are involved with remarriage, such as alimony, child support, and division of property from former marriages. Many other people are involved directly or indirectly, such as former spouses and his, her, and their children. Remarried individuals frequently take on an additional family. Given that the state does not issue guidelines for establishing rights and responsibilities pertaining to such considerations as pension rights, medical coverage, and life insurance, important questions need to be settled by the couple.

Project. Interview a few individuals who have been remarried. Try to develop a diverse sample in terms of age, gender, and other characteristics. Develop questions ahead of time that reflect each of the six areas listed. Avoid yes or no questions; rather, ask open-ended questions. Describe your sample (age, gender, ethnicity, income and education level, etc.), report your findings, and discuss whether the participants' diversity affected the findings and how they compare to what Goetting presents.

Sample.

Source of this section is Ann Goetting, "The Six Stations of Remarriage: Developmental Tasks for Remarriage after Divorce," *Family Relations 32,* no. 2 (April 1982).

Findings.

Discussion.

(Attach another sheet of paper if needed.)

ANSWER KEY

Key Terms

1. blended family
2. complex stepfamily
3. Pseudomutuality
4. Stepping Ahead Program
5. Joint custody
6. stepfamily
7. Remarriage
8. simple stepfamily
9. stepparent
10. sole custody
11. PREPARE-MC
12. binuclear family
13. split custody

Multiple Choice

1. d
2. b
3. a
4. b
5. d
6. c
7. c
8. d
9. b
10. c
11. a
12. b
13. c
14. d
15. d

True/False

1. F
2. F
3. T
4. T
5. T
6. F
7. F
8. T
9. T
10. T

Suggested Responses to Short Answer Questions

1. 1) Perfect pals, 2) cooperative colleagues, 3) angry associates, and 4) fiery foes.

2. 1) Mothers with sole custody; 2) fathers with sole custody; 3) split-custody families, in which the father has sole custody of one or more children and the mother has sole custody of one or more children; and 4) joint-custody families, in which the mother and the father share decision making.

3. 1) Entering a new relationship: one should have recovered from the loss of the first marriage and have recommitted to the institution of marriage itself; 2) planning the new marriage and family: one should have accepted the fears of all members of the new family about forming a stepfamily as well as have accepted the time and patience required to adjust to the realities of the new family; 3) marriage and reconstitution of the family: the new partners must view the new marriage and the new stepfamily as genuine and positive, with a restructuring of the new relationships.

4. 1) Biological parent-child ties; 2) the nature and length of the couple's marriage; 3) parent-child emotional bonds; 4) loyalty issues; 5) extended-family issues; 6) struggles between children; and 7) the degree of demand on financial resources.

5. 1) Limited money, often exacerbated by lack of or limited child support; 2) loneliness; 3) work overload; 4) continued conflict with ex-spouse.

CHAPTER 18

STRENGTHENING FAMILIES IN THE FUTURE

CHAPTER OUTLINE

The Future of Families from a Global Perspective

The Future of Your Family

Strengthening Your Marriage and Family Relationships
    Personal Strategies
    Programs for Couples and Families
    Premarital Counseling and Couple Enrichment
    Marriage Enrichment Programs
    Marital and Family Therapy
    Using the Family Circumplex Model in Family Therapy

2001: Recommendations for Strengthening Marriages and Families

Making Every Year the International Year of the Family

LEARNING OBJECTIVES

After reading Chapter 18, you should be able to:
- Discuss how diversity does not have to be a problem in society but can be a source of strength
- Explain the development of the concept of the universality of human nature
- Discuss the common qualities of strong families around the world
- Explain the significance of the Gaia hypothesis for families
- Discuss the variety of programs to help people deal successfully with couple and family problems
- Outline some of the major problems families face today in the United States and around the world, and discuss how we can all work together toward solutions

PRACTICE TESTS

Key Terms

1. The "four great virtues" that Boulding describes as being part of the "ultimate good" may be considered as _____.

2. The concept of the _____ contrasts with the notion of cultural uniqueness.

3. The _____ is reflected in the bumper sticker "Think globally and act locally."

4. _____ can be a cost-effective and efficient approach to resolve emotional and relationship problems in families.

5. _____ programs can assist couples who have a good marriage improve their marriage and/or learn communication skills.

Multiple Choice

1. George Homans believed that certain societal institutions appear in every culture because of the:
   a. importance of biopsychosocial social theory
   b. universality of human nature
   c. Gaia hypothesis
   d. notion that we are all brothers (and sisters)

2. All of the following are similar qualities the authors believe are shared by strong and successful families around the world EXCEPT:
   a. cohesion
   b. flexibility
   c. stability
   d. communication

3. The Gaia hypothesis was inspired by:
   a. the first photographs of Earth from space
   b. *in utero* photographs of a developing baby
   c. the Greek myth that the Earth is our mother
   d. the discovery of DNA

4. Doherty and Simmons's national survey of marital and family therapists and a sampling of their clients found the most common presenting problem of their clients to be associated with:
   a. marital problems
   b. alcohol/drugs
   c. depression
   d. parent-child problems

5. Overall, _____ percent of clients surveyed in Doherty and Simmons's national survey of marital and family therapy practices indicated that their therapeutic goals had been achieved.
   a. 25
   b. 42
   c. 67
   d. 83

6. Studies of thousands of strong families indicate that to succeed in difficult times in life, a family must:
   a. look for something positive in the difficult situation
   b. pull together
   c. find the person who is the source of the problem
   d. a and b

7. Even though it does not fit every such family, "problem" families are generally defined as:
   a. those that do not function well
   b. those that are extreme on one or both dimensions of the Family Circumplex Model
   c. those that are voluntarily or involuntarily involved in a treatment program
   d. all of the above

8. According to Hamilton S. McCubbin, in the 21st century _____ percent of the U.S. population will be people of color.
   a. 13
   b. 23
   c. 33
   d. 43

9. According to Murray A. Straus, what has decreased the rate of spouse and child abuse over the past decade?
   a. shelters and severe penalties for abuse
   b. shelters and treatment programs
   c. a nationwide campaign aimed at educating the public on the dangers of abuse
   d. all of the above

10. According to Murray A. Straus, over _____ children and _____ spouses are abused physically each year.
    a. six million; three million
    b. ten million; eight million
    c. one million; five million
    d. 800,000; two million

11. According to Carlfred Broderick, "The future of marital and family therapy lies in the replacement of _____ with a tested set of broadly accepted principles of systemic intervention having specific components and therapeutic behaviors."
    a. family systems theory
    b. cognitive dissonance theory
    c. competing therapies
    d. all of the above

12. Which of the following was NOT one of the six objectives developed for the International Year of the Family at the 1994 United Nations conference?
    a. Increase awareness of family issues among governments and the private sector.
    b. Encourage the private sector to take over many of the functions of government that are overly costly for taxpayers.
    c. Stimulate response to problems affecting and affected by the situations of families.
    d. Encourage national institutions to formulate, implement, and monitor family policies.

13. Which issue did Bert Adams, in the National Council on Family Relations Presidential Report, *2001*, refer to its infrastructure as being large and growing in a relatively haphazard, unplanned manner?
    a. child care
    b. elder care
    c. health care
    d. alcohol and other substance-abuse treatment programs

14. Which of the following is generally NOT considered to be an essential component of effective premarital programs?
    a. a premarital inventory with individual feedback for each couple
    b. skill building focusing on communication and problem-solving skills
    c. a small group in which couples can discuss mutual issues
    d. analysis of strengths and weaknesses of each partner's family of origin

15. Which type of marriage enrichment program has been found overall to be the most helpful for couples?
    a. couple enrichment
    b. skill building
    c. conflict resolution
    d. "learning to live together"

True/False

1. As presented in the text, strong families are families without problems.
2. Most research conducted on families has focused on dysfunctional and problem families.
3. The Gaia hypothesis was inspired by the first photographs of a baby *in utero*.
4. Most people seek help for family problems before they become severe.
5. Funding support has been fairly even for research on problems in families as well as on strengths of families.
6. Overall, similarities are more prevalent than differences among strong families across various ethnic groups.
7. Effective marital and family therapy lasts for longer periods of time relative to the more traditional individual therapy provided by psychiatrists and psychologists.
8. The strongest families are those that reach outside the family for help—e.g., to marriage and family therapists—rather than relying on family members for help.
9. Communication in strong families is always of a positive nature.
10. Families that are strong and successful around the world are likely to share similar qualities: cohesion, commitment, and flexibility.

Short Answer

1. Identify the three essential components of an effective premarital program.

2. Discuss the potential benefits of marital and family therapy.

3. Identify three guidelines suggested by the authors to use in selecting a marriage and family therapist.

4. Identify and describe the three qualities likely shared by strong and successful families around the world.

5. Identify four key points, and the president who made each, that were included in the NCFR Presidential Report, *2001: Preparing Families for the Future*.

Name _____   Chapter 18

PERSONAL INVOLVEMENT ASSESSMENT—
MARRIAGE QUIZ

Jerry Larson, a marriage and family therapist, developed this Marriage Quiz for students in his family life courses at Brigham Young University and for use in his premarital counseling. Take the quiz yourself and then compare your score with those of Larson's 279 unmarried undergraduates who also took the quiz. Each question should be answered as either true or false. The answers, which are given on page 218, are based on findings from various research studies.

_____ 1. Husbands are happier when their wives are homemakers rather than employed full-time.

_____ 2. Most young, single, never-married people will eventually get married.

_____ 3. Having a child usually improves marital satisfaction for both spouses.

_____ 4. The best single predictor of marital satisfaction is the quality of a couple's sex life.

_____ 5. The U.S. divorce rate rose between 1960 and 1980.

_____ 6. There are more two-career couples now than in 1970.

_____ 7. If my spouse loves me, he or she should instinctively know what I want and need to be happy.

_____ 8. Wives are usually less satisfied in marriage when they fill the roles of both homemaker and full-time employee.

_____ 9. When the wife is employed outside the home full-time, the husband usually assumes an equal share of the housekeeping.

_____ 10. Couples' marital satisfaction usually increases gradually from the first year of marriage through the child-bearing years, the teen years, the empty-nest period, and retirement.

_____ 11. No matter how I behave, my spouse should love me simply because he or she is my spouse.

_____ 12. One of the most frequent problems couples face is poor communication.

_____ 13. Husbands usually make more life-style adjustments in marriage than wives do.

_____ 14. Couples who live together before marriage usually report greater marital satisfaction than couples who do not.

_____ 15. I can change my spouse by pointing out his or her inadequacies, errors, etc.

_____ 16. Divorce is more likely if the couple married before the age of 18.

_____ 17. My spouse either loves me or doesn't; nothing I do will affect this.

_____ 18. The more spouses disclose positive and negative information to each other, the greater the satisfaction.

_____ 19. I must feel better about my partner before I can change my behavior toward him or her.

_____ 20. Maintaining romantic love is the key to a satisfying and enduring marriage.

Pamela Adelman, "Marital Myths: What We Know Hurts," *Psychology Today,* May 1989, pp. 68, 70. Reprinted with permission from Psychology Today Magazine. Copyright © 1989 Sussex Publishers, Inc.

Answers. All false except for numbers 2, 5, 6, 12, and 16.

Larson's students' results: On the average, Larson's students thought almost half of the false statements were true. The women generally did better than the men which, according to Larson, probably indicates "socialization, which encourages women to think about and prepare more for marriage than men." But both men and women believed some myths; for example, more than 75 percent agreed that increased self-disclosure enhances marital satisfaction for both partners, regardless of whether it is positive or negative self-disclosure (the statement is true only if self-disclosure is mostly positive). Fortunately, some of Larson's students improved their scores after completing a course on marriage and the family. Which means, of course, that yours should be fairly high by now!

Comparison of your score with those of Larson's students.

Name _____   Chapter 18

KNOWLEDGE IN ACTION—
PROMOTING EFFECTIVE LEGISLATION FOR CHILDREN AND FAMILIES[1]

Chapter 18 includes a synopsis of recommendations concerning the future of families, made by nineteen renowned family scholars, thirteen of whom are former presidents of the National Council on Family Relations (NCFR). Their recommendations were included in a NCFR Presidential Report, *2001: Preparing Families for the Future* (Olson and Hanson, 1990). Whether the issue focused on was single parents, health care, child care, divorce, family violence, alcohol/substance abuse, marital and parent-child conflict, AIDS, family sexual health, or other issues, these experts called for a higher priority on families in developing social policies. Olson, one of the former NCFR presidents, as well as co-editor of the publication and coauthor of this text, indicates that one way to make families a national priority is to develop a family impact statement for every major piece of legislation at the local, state, and national level. Doing so would provide for policies that would be more humane as well as more effective in serving individual and family needs.

What does go on with public policy development through legislation? In 1995, the State Legislative Leaders Foundation, with the support of the Annie E. Casey and Ford Foundations, published its report, *State Legislative Leaders: Keys to Effective Legislation for Children and Families*. The report summarizes the findings from interviews conducted with 177 influential Republican and Democratic state legislative leaders from all 50 states. In addition, the report includes findings from 167 questionnaires responded to by representatives of child and family organizations that engage in advocacy and legislative lobbying efforts.

The key findings of the study are:

1. Although state legislative leaders mainly focus on managing the legislative process and on the state budget, they are increasingly speaking out on major public policy issues.

2. The importance of child and family issues varies by state and by leader.

3. State legislative leaders' knowledge of children and family policies and programs is limited and often based on anecdotes.

4. State legislative leaders see no clear discernible legislative agenda nor advocacy structure for children and families.

5. Children and family advocates appear to be too liberal and Democratic to suit most legislative leaders.

6. Leaders are unaware of any cohesive, effective grassroots constituency concerned with children and family issues.

7. Leaders understand the roles of lobbyists better than they do the roles of advocates, who they often perceive as "elitists" who view the legislative process and legislators negatively.

8. Leaders view some of the strategies used by children and family advocates as irrelevant or counterproductive, e.g., "Children's Day" rallies.

9. Children and family advocacy groups need training, funding, and flexibility in order to develop and implement effective strategies essential to legislative success.

10. Legislative leaders should become more proactive in seeking out information on children and family issues.

---

[1] Material in this section comes from *State Legislative Leaders: Keys to Effective Legislation for Children and Families—A Report,* State Legislative Leaders Foundation, 16 Bayberry Square, 1645 Falmouth Rd., Centerville, MA 02632, 1995.

Project. While the report has to do with public policy at the *state* level, public policy is also enacted legislatively at the federal (Congress) and local levels (county councils, city councils, school boards, etc.). There are *two options* for this project, both of which require interviewing individuals involved with public policy: either *policymakers* (e.g., school board, city council, or county council members; state legislators; members of Congress) or children and family *advocates*. If you are unable to interview elected officials themselves, you may interview members of their staffs.

Procedure. Prepare some questions ahead of time that pertain to the findings of the legislative leaders report. Then call offices of a few of your elected representatives, asking to interview them. (You can find names and phone numbers in the front of your telephone directory under the "Government Pages" listing or through the county records and elections division.) Or, for the second option, call offices of children and family advocacy groups. (You can find organizations listed at the front of the phone book under a "Community Service Numbers" listing.) Try to get three interviews if possible. Conduct your interviews by phone or in person. Summarize your findings and contrast them with those from the legislative leaders report.

Sample. (Persons interviewed)

Questions Asked.

Summary/Discussion.

ANSWER KEY

Key Terms

1. universal values
2. universality of human nature
3. Gaia hypothesis
4. marital and family therapy
5. marriage enrichment

Multiple Choice

1. b	6. d	11. c
2. c	7. c	12. b
3. a	8. c	13. a
4. c	9. b	14. d
5. d	10. a	15. b

True/False

1. F	6. T
2. T	7. F
3. F	8. F
4. F	9. F
5. F	10. F

Suggested Responses to Short Answer Questions

1. 1) A premarital inventory with individual feedback for each couple; 2) skill building that focuses on communication and problem-solving skills; and 3) a small group for the couples to discuss their mutual interests.

2. It is relatively short term compared to traditional individual therapy, it is rather cost effective and efficient, and the outcome is usually very successful based on both the clients, and therapist's perspective.

3. 1) Check professional credentials and experience; 2) consult qualified referral services and agencies; and 3) ask questions about the therapy, the therapist's professional training and educational background, etc.

4. 1) *cohesion:* a scene of togetherness, a commitment to each other demonstrated by satisfying times spent with each other in the family; 2) *flexibility:* the ability to successfully meet the minor and major stressors of life; founded on a shared set of common goals, values, and beliefs which give family members a sense of spiritual well-being; and 3) *communication:* the capacity to listen and talk effectively with each other and to express appreciation and affection for all family members.

5. 1) Families must be a national priority (Olson); 2) families are diverse in terms of ethnicity, family dynamics, and types of structures (Olson, Rubin); 3) the United States in the 21st century will have greater ethnic diversity (McCubbin); 4) It is difficult to develop generalities that apply to every type of family as families have changed so much (Glick); 5) there is an increasing need for dependent-care programs and many working families are responsible for elder care and child care simultaneously (Voydanoff); 6) families are increasingly experiencing economic challenges (Hogan); 7) health care is a growing problem for families (Gilliss); 8) continuing education for families on AIDS prevention and help is needed (Needle); 9) "family sexual health" should be an important concept among policy makers (Maddock); 10) variation by gender in families still exists (Walker); 11) child-care planning and support are needed (Adams); 12) resources are needed for emotional, financial, housing, and health support for older family members (Force); 13) there needs to be more learning about the dynamics underlying healthy family relationships (Spanier); 14) the reality of divorce as a viable family transition needs to be accepted (Price); 15) family violence continues, and clear national policies and programs are needed to help (Straus); 16) an all-out war against drug abuse is needed (Lewis); etc.